WRITING THEMSELVES
INTO THE MOVEMENT

A Volume in the Series

CHILDHOODS: INTERDISCIPLINARY
PERSPECTIVES ON CHILDREN AND YOUTH

Edited by

Karen Sánchez-Eppler, Rachel Conrad,
Laura L. Lovett, and Alice Hearst

WRITING THEMSELVES INTO THE MOVEMENT

CHILD AUTHORS
OF THE BLACK
ARTS ERA   AMY FISH

UNIVERSITY OF MASSACHUSETTS PRESS
Amherst and Boston

ISBN 978-1-62534-826-5 (paper); 827-2 (hardcover)

Designed by Sally Nichols
Set in Adobe Jenson Pro
Printed and bound by Books International, Inc.

Cover design by adam b. bohannon
Cover photo by June Jordan,
Young Girl Writing, 1972. Courtesy June M. Jordan
Literary Estate Trust.

Library of Congress Cataloging-in-Publication Data

Names: Fish, Amy, 1986- author.
Title: Writing themselves into the movement : child authors of the Black
Arts era / Amy Fish.
Description: Amherst : University of Massachusetts Press, 2024. | Series:
Childhoods: interdisciplinary perspectives on children and youth |
Includes bibliographical references and index. |
Identifiers: LCCN 2024029881 (print) | LCCN 2024029882 (ebook) | ISBN
9781625348265 (paperback) | ISBN 9781625348272 (hardcover) | ISBN
9781685750978 (ebook) | ISBN 9781685750985 (epub)
Subjects: LCSH: Children's writings, American—New York (State)—New
York—History and criticism. | American literature—Minority
authors—History and criticism. | LCGFT: Literary criticism.
Classification: LCC PS153.C44 F57 2024 (print) | LCC PS153.C44 (ebook) |
DDC 810.9/99282—dc23/eng/20240830
LC record available at https://lccn.loc.gov/2024029881
LC ebook record available at https://lccn.loc.gov/2024029882

British Library Cataloguing-in-Publication Data
A catalog record for this book is available from the British Library.

Christopher Meyer, "Wonderful New York," in Jordan and Bush, *Voice of the Children*, 11.
© Christopher D. Meyer, 1970. Reprinted by permission of the Frances Goldin Literary Agency.

June Jordan to "Visitors and Adult Friends of the Children," 1969–70, June Jordan Papers,
Box 54. © Christopher D. Meyer, 1970. All rights reserved. Reprinted by permission
of the Frances Goldin Literary Agency.

June Jordan to Zelda Wirtshafter, February 12, 1968, in Lopate, *Journal of a Living Experiment*, 146.
© Christopher D. Meyer, 1979. All rights reserved. Reprinted by permission of the
Frances Goldin Literary Agency.

Contents

List of Illustrations

Acknowledgments

Several authors and collaborators of 1960s–1970s youth writing have encouraged my research and shared their memories, insights, and documents with me. I am honored to have connected with these people: former child author, lifelong poet, and educator Yolanda Prescott; former child author and financial services professional Michelle Smith Jones; educators Elaine Avidon and Marvin Hoffman; photographer Anna Winand; and novelist, playwright, and former teacher Irving Benig. For permissions related to *The Me Nobody Knows* musical, I thank Courtney Holt, who shared the work of lyricist Will Holt, and composer Gary William Friedman, who kindly corresponded with me, and whose music has given lasting theatrical life to youth writing. I am indebted to those who have worked to enable my archival research and shared their knowledge and materials, particularly the staffs of the Schlesinger Library at the Harvard Radcliffe Institute, Harvard University; the Special Collections Research Center at Syracuse University; the Billy Rose Theatre Division, the Berg Collection, and the Permissions and Reproduction office of the New York Public Library; and the Teachers & Writers Collaborative.

This project began as a dissertation directed by Robin Bernstein, who makes mentorship into an art. Robin and my committee, Glenda Carpio, Doris Sommer, and Katharine Capshaw, vitally shaped this project; my reading, writing, and teaching; and my awareness of the significance and beauty of everyday life. Many cases of writer's block were evaded by opening Kate's *Civil Rights Childhood* next to me. My phenomenal fellow American studies graduate students, including Rebecca Scofield, John Frederick Bell, and Michael King, and our peerless administrator, Arthur Patton-Hock, taught me much about work and play. I thank Harvard University for funding my doctoral studies.

I am proud to call Boston University's Kilachand Honors College my academic home, during and after my postdoctoral fellowship. Kilachand has spoiled me for colleagues and students. Every one of my fellow postdocs and office mates has made my work better and my days happier. Among these friends, Travis Franks, Danielle Drees, and Can Evren provided astute feedback on this work. I have been exquisitely supported by the remarkable Carrie Preston, Linda Doerrer, Joanna Davidson, Anna Henchman, and Melissa Holt.

This work benefited from exchanges at the Children and Youth Studies Caucus of the American Studies Association, the Children's Literature Association, the Society for the History of Childhood and Youth, and Modern Language Association. Thank you to my interlocutors and to the people who sustain and strengthen these organizations. I am grateful to the scholars who mentored and inspired this study and whose own books I continually revisit, including Marah Gubar, Kevin Quashie, Michelle Martin, Marilisa Jiménez García, Ju Yon Kim, Victoria Ford Smith, and Robert B. Stepto. I thank Philip Nel for this book's title, among other gifts.

My series editors, Rachel Conrad and Karen Sánchez-Eppler, have graciously allowed me to call on their expertise throughout the making of this book. I am grateful for their examples and kindness. Matt Becker and his colleagues at the University of Massachusetts Press have steered me with warmth and acumen. My anonymous readers' perceptive feedback and generous suggestions greatly strengthened this work. Timothy Lundy's editorial skill was crucial to the final revisions. I thank Ivo Fravashi for copyediting and Sandy Sadow for compiling the index. Portions of chapter 3 and the epilogue are revised from "Agency in Absentia: Child Authorship under Racial Oppression in *The Me Nobody Knows*," *The Lion and the Unicorn* 44, no. 1 (January 2020): 56–77; my thanks to Karin Westman, the anonymous reviewers of the article, and Johns Hopkins University Press.

I thank my parents: my dad, who treats learning as an adventure and precision as an act of love; and my mom, English teacher to thousands of young people, devourer of stories and art, book fairy to two lucky grandchildren, and always my first reader. Cesarina Calderón and Sandra Medina made this book possible by providing exceptional care to my children. Among the friends who keep me nourished: Adriane Levin, Nisha Gadgil, Lindsay Laguna, Emily

MacMillan, and Yoona Kim, thank you. Samir, I was beginning this project when we met. Thank you for believing in me, for caring for me, for giving me a dream extended family, and for making life good. Raia and Kavi, my hands may often be too full to type, but my heart is too full to mind.

The work of June Jordan has shaped every stage and page of this project, including the book cover, which features her photography. This book is dedicated to Jordan and to the child authors discussed here.

WRITING THEMSELVES
INTO THE MOVEMENT

A Youth Writing Movement

I'm sitting here on the floor ready to write a composition with my best friend Carmen and then all of a sudden we started to laugh and say how good it is to be poor. . . . Being poor and honest, without showing off or just trying to be rich and greedy with your money will let you have fun in this world and you won't let yourself be swallowed by wealth.

You don't have to separate yourself from this life that tries to lock you in it. . . . I'm telling you that's why I don't feel so bad about being poor.

—Elisa, Lower East Side, New York, 1967–68

Between 1967 and 1972, a previously obscure group of authors entered the US cultural spotlight. In this five-year period alone, at least thirty anthologies of poetry and prose by children, specifically African American, Latinx, Asian American, and Native American children, poured from adult-led workshops, classrooms, and carceral spaces. Volumes emerged from mass-market publishers, independent imprinters, and local mimeograph machines. These anthologies attracted attention from such luminaries as James Baldwin, sometimes became bestsellers, and even inspired a hit Broadway musical. With titles such as *I Am Somebody!* and *The Me Nobody Knows: Children's Voices from the Ghetto*, youth writing collections trumpeted the arrival of a long-suppressed American voice. This voice attracted a broad swath of readers, spanning age, race, ethnicity, class, and region. While writings by children had long attracted adult attention, the circa-1970 moment was distinguished by the widespread belief that children of color from poor and working-class neighborhoods were uniquely able to speak truth about American racism and inequality.

This surge of attention receives playful treatment in sixth grader Elisa's ode to being "poor and honest," which opens this introduction.[1] The writer's position on the floor grounds her warmly personal use of the first and second persons, performing humility with assurance. The friends' maxim "how good it is to be poor" asserts their literary authority within their specific class position. The friends claim moral force with the simple phrase "how good." Yet Elisa also destabilizes this regard for poverty through the friends' sudden laughter. Their amusement suggests that the friends may be satirically indulging a privileged adult appetite for oppressed children's voices. Elisa thus anticipates the success of the anthology that features her prose, *Can't You Hear Me Talking to You?*, the popular 1971 collection of largely Puerto Rican children's writings from one Lower East Side school. Elisa and Carmen's moment of laughter initiates the only use of the past tense in the passage: "all of a sudden we *started* to laugh" (italics mine). The use of the past tense, a mark of conventional storytelling, locates the origin of the narrative act in the moment of laughing recognition. This temporal break marks the surrounding stream-of-consciousness present tense as artifice: Elisa is not an ethnographic subject but an active artist. In her account, literary creation stems directly from the girls' critical attention to their circumstances. Elisa constantly announces her own narrative act and its effect on her audience: "I'm sitting here. . . . I'm telling you." Her self-conscious scene of composition calls attention to the human experience of writing, a process simultaneously comical, painful, and tender.

In the anthology *Can't You Hear Me Talking to You?*, the prose of Elisa and her peers was edited and laden with commentary by a white teacher. This mediation typifies the constrained circumstances of literary publication for children of the 1960s and 1970s. While young people have always found ways to make art among themselves and away from adults, popular anthologies of this era were created on less autonomous terms. Adults, often white and middle-class, prompted and coached children's work and provided space, time, and paper for writing. Some adult collaborators managed wholehearted aid and advocacy with minimal interference in the writing process. These adults considered themselves necessary liaisons to the adult world for the children, who were truly in charge. As Elaine Avidon, adviser to the youth writing collective What's Happening, recalls, "The kids owned this."[2] Still, adults commonly corrected perceived errors in children's writing, collected and arranged pieces for anthologies, and provided the editorial commentaries and publicity that framed readers' understandings of children's words. The power difference between young writers and older collaborators carried real stakes. Children were vulnerable to white adults both directly and through institutions such as schools, child welfare departments, and courts. Young writers might derive satisfaction and recognition from being published or find their writings distorted by editing and paratextual framing. With little ownership over their works, children might receive scholarships and other forms of profit sharing from publication or nothing at all.

These uncertainties raised questions for contemporaneous readers that remain salient today. Should we dismiss youth writing anthologies as hopelessly mediated or accept them as true reflections of children's agency? Elisa's self-conscious vignette suggests a third approach: centering children's own critical perspectives on their authorship. I argue that children themselves address the challenge of interpreting marginalized young people's traces in the archives. Focusing on anthologized texts written by primarily Black and Puerto Rican young people in New York City schools, community programs, and carceral spaces, I read children as theorists of literary voice, who turn constrained conditions of authorship into occasions of social critique and self-discovery. Elisa and her peers collectively develop a set of rhetorical strategies that self-consciously examine the dynamics of authorship and readership in a society shaped by inequalities of age, race, ethnicity, class, and gender. These literary tactics not only negotiate white adult control but also open space for young writers' self-witness: the practice of observing and testing one's own capacities, possibilities, tastes, and personal ties in ways that both confront and surpass the terms of power.

Though broadly impactful, circa-1970 children's writings have fallen into obscurity, remaining largely excluded from our narratives of the era's literature, culture, and politics. Close attention to a specific time and place—New York City in the late 1960s and early 1970s—reveals how child authors wrote themselves into the era's cultural and political movements in multiple ways. In particular, young writers were active participants in the East Coast wing of the Black Arts Movement, a cultural nationalist project that pursued liberation through Black art forms. At the same time, child authors of circa-1970 New York constituted a distinct, youth-specific literary movement, with its own forms, tropes, and patterns of production and readership. Finally, young people of the era developed ways to write themselves: to experiment with self-definition through writing and to find ways of setting their own creative terms, even under adult supervision. Child authors of the Black Arts era bend the opportunities and tensions of compromised authorship to their own expressive ends.

UNEQUAL COLLABORATION: AN AMERICAN GENRE

Writing Themselves into the Movement claims circa-1970 children's place within a lineage of marginalized American writers who have negotiated more powerful collaborators, including slave narrative authors with white publishers or amanuenses, Indigenous creators of "told-to" narratives, and women censored by men. Mediated texts, argues Sophie McCall, can "challenge notions of 'voice' that are singular, unmediated, and pure"—disrupting, in Christine Cavalier's words, the "binary-driven discourse with which critics have opposed collaboration to subversion."[3] The paradigm of collaboration draws together seemingly unrelated texts—in this case, relating child authors of circa-1970 New York to Canadian Aboriginal texts (in McCall's study) and a nineteenth-century Native woman writer (in Cavalier's essay). Such links reveal the broad scale of unequal collaboration as a genre rooted in the Americas' histories of conquest, genocide, enslavement, resistance, and liberation. Texts that show the tampering fingerprints of power help build an accurate and inclusive picture of American literature and reveal the ways in which art takes shape in an unequal world. Childhood offers a vivid perspective on these compromised terms. As Karen Sánchez-Eppler argues, "Children's dependent state embodies a mode of identity, or relation to family, institution, or nation, that may indeed offer a more accurate and productive model for social interaction than the ideal autonomous individual of liberalism's rights discourse ever has."[4] Overtly mediated literature authored by children can sensitize us to the messy influences, collaborations, and inequities behind apparently autonomously authored works. The genre of unequal collaboration sparks the question: who can tell the story of America?

The entanglement of mediation, childhood, and American literature has a long history, exemplified by the reception of Phillis Wheatley, an artistic ancestor of circa-1970 youth writers. As an enslaved African girl in Revolutionary Boston, Wheatley was permitted to publish her poetry only after a jury of eighteen prominent white men interrogated her to assess whether she actually could have written her heralded verses. The men's endorsement would grace the opening pages of her 1773 book. Wheatley went back on trial two centuries later, when several Black Arts Movement writers scorned her as a sellout with a "white mind."[5] Questioned first for her veracity and then for her authenticity, Wheatley demonstrates the interpretive bind of mediated authors—a bind tightened by marginalized identities of age, race, and gender. Despite their disparagement, Black Arts writers frequently included Wheatley in anthologies of the period in a kind of paradoxical act of recovery.[6] The drive to reckon with Wheatley, however negatively, demonstrates youth writing's importance as a site for both young and adult thinkers to work through concepts of artistic voice, authenticity, and self-determination. Poet, activist, and educator June Jordan, whose collaborations with young writers are central to this book, would embrace the complexity of Wheatley's authorship in a 1986 essay. Wheatley, Jordan writes, manifests the "difficult miracle" by which constrained and unfree Black artists nevertheless create poetry, fundamentally a genre of freedom—thus declaring themselves both incompletely and fully "at liberty," incompletely and fully "at home."[7]

Recognizing unequal collaboration as an American genre, stretching from Wheatley's 1770s to Elisa's 1960s, reveals that authorship is not a stable category but rather a field of possibilities shaped by social circumstances. To write for any kind of audience is to enter into social negotiation, and that process is made particularly vivid by children's minor status. Young writers' histories of unequal collaboration reveal how the forces that have shaped the Americas have also shaped the nature of literature on this terrain. The very concepts of authorship, of literary value, and of public voice are defined by American structures of power and by individual artists' creative negotiations of those conditions.

Still, the study of unequally collaborative texts raises compelling objections. Don't Black and Puerto Rican young writers deserve to be heard on their own terms, without constant reference to the intrusions of white adults? More broadly, comparing children to slave narrative authors and other adult writers may raise concerns about the racist infantilization of non-white adults. The paradigm of collaboration can euphemize unequal power relations or, conversely, overemphasize the limits of marginalized writers' creative agency—in both cases reducing authors to the terms of their constraints. White men, meanwhile, regularly enjoy coaching, editing, and cowriting contributions from others yet tend to receive sole authorial credit. In this light, dwelling on apparently tainted works of minority literature, those arguably designed to turn a profit for white editors and publishers—particularly in the late twentieth century, which offers a wealth of more freely authored texts—may seem to undermine youth voice rather than honor it.

A rare scholarly discussion of 1960s–1970s youth anthologies both raises this challenge and hints at a response. In a searing single paragraph on the subject, historian Robin D. G. Kelley recalls his own recruitment as a child writer within white liberal practices of cultural exploitation:

> Even our liberal white teachers who were committed to making us into functional members of society turned out to be foot soldiers in the new eth-nographic army. With the overnight success of published collections of inner city children's writings like *The Me Nobody Knows* and Caroline Mirthes's *Can't You Hear Me Talking to You?*, writing about the intimate details of our home life seemed like our most important assignment. (And we made the most of it by enriching our mundane narratives with stories from *Mod Squad, Hawaii Five-O*, and *Speed Racer*.) . . . White America's fascination with the pathological urban poor translated into massive book sales.[8]

Kelley categorizes youth anthologies—including the volume featuring Elisa—as part of a broad rejuvenation of white consumption and control of poor neighborhoods on post–civil rights terms. The military image of "the new ethnographic army" connects the War on Poverty to US military aggression in Vietnam. Kelley's naming of "our most important assignment" closes the distance between the scholastic and military meanings of *assignment*. The reference to "overnight success" connotes not only speed but also the extension of white surveillance into the most "intimate" hours of family and community life, and particularly into the lives of Black young people. This process of surveillance and extraction could operate powerfully through the collection of children's writings.

Even while skewering the youth writing trend, Kelley points the way toward a recuperative, child-centered reading. In a pointed parenthetical, the work of "the new ethnographic army" comes under covert attack by children themselves. Appropriating plot points from popular TV shows, including police dramas, young writers present themselves as observers and consumers, not merely the observed and the consumed. The same children whose writings bring "massive book sales" advance their own definition of profit by "enriching" their life writings. Placing essential meaning in parenthetical enclosure, Kelley locates children's literary stories outside of dominant narratives. His rhetori-cal playfulness registers a pulse of creative energy that exceeds the bounds of white adult control, constructing a canny, irreverent collective children's voice that resonates with Elisa and Carmen's knowing laughter. Such moments of children's knowing offer both a warning and an invitation for study. As a white adult scholar, I risk reproducing the exploitative modes of attention that Kelley exposes. Young writers point the way to avoid this pitfall, crafting inventive ways of confronting questions of authenticity, contingency, and complicity—even as they also make meaning beyond these terms and turn their uneven circumstances to their personal expressive ends.

My analysis of young writers' theoretical work is indebted to the methods of historians of Black girlhood, childhood, and youth, who have uncovered traces of young people's interiority and creativity within heavily mediated sources, such as sociological interviews and court records. Rather than scrutinizing children's agency or authenticity, these historians recognize young people as active shapers of the cultural category of childhood, canny navigators of power dynamics and investigators of their own inner lives. As Paula C. Austin characterizes young participants in midcentury sociological studies, historical Black youth have been "thinkers, theorists, critics, and commentators as they reckoned with, reconciled, and even played with the material and rhetorical lines of demarcation set about them" by age, gender, race, and class.[9] The methodological innovations of Austin and other twenty-first-century historians enable attention to cases of child authorship heavily marked by white and/or adult power, far from the best-case scenario of sensitive adult collaboration. Applying Austin's framework to a corpus of youth writing, I ask how children conceive of their own authorship and examine the possibilities for unfolding their inner lives on the page even through mediated forms. This perspective draws on an intellectual tradition of recognizing Black children's theoretical practices. As bell hooks would write in 1991 of her 1950s–1960s childhood, "I found a place of sanctuary in 'theorizing,' in making sense out of what was happening. I found a place where I could imagine possible futures, a place where life could be lived differently."[10]

Attention to children's self-theorizing aligns with a growing current within scholarship on Black childhood and Black studies at large, which seeks to move beyond a sole focus on paradigms of resistance and toward frameworks of interiority, relationality, and capacious being. Kevin Quashie's theories of "black aliveness" and "black quiet" shape my vocabulary of interiority and train my focus on children's meanings beyond public imperatives.[11] Attention to children's collaborations and constraints need not reduce youth artistry to the terms of power—to a view of children as always speaking toward, away from, around, or otherwise in relation to a white adult reader. Rather, young writers turn the opportunities and tensions of compromised authorship to their own purposes. Behold Elisa, enraptured by her own act of writing and by her conspiratorial closeness to her friend Carmen. Child writers stage encounters with their own capacities and eccentricities, solitude and intimacies, lived experiences and imagined alternatives.

CHILD AUTHORS IN THE BLACK ARTS MOVEMENT

Children's investigations of authorship are a little-recognized site of 1960s–1970s thought about self-determination and artistic freedom. In particular, young writers of circa-1970 New York City were vital interlocutors of the Black Arts Movement. Generally periodized from 1965 to 1975, the Black Arts Movement was a wide-ranging flourishing of writers and artists working to produce, share, and theorize art that was rooted in African diasporic experience, language, and cultural forms; that imagined and sought creatively to enact Black liberation; and that engaged with the radical political ideas of the Black Power Movement, including cultural nationalism and self-determination. The Black Arts Movement was markedly regional, with distinct East Coast and West Coast characters as well as additional centers of national importance, such as Detroit. James Smethurst emphasizes the "dynamic instability" of New York's Black Arts scene, as the city failed to cultivate the same level of enduring Black Arts presses, galleries, and theaters formed elsewhere.[12] Still, New York was home to short-lived but influential institutions and leading Black Arts creators—many of whom associated with young writers, as I discuss throughout this book. Perhaps the decentralized, constantly shifting Black Arts scene in the city opened space for young people to join the action. New York, moreover, was the heart of Puerto Rican Black Arts activity. Artists of Puerto Rican descent variously participated in the Black Arts Movement and exchanged ideas with it, crucially contributing to the flourishing of Nuyorican poetry as well as subsequent decades of multicultural literary activity.[13] As a movement of primarily Black and Puerto Rican young people, circa-1970 youth writing helped shape New York's multicultural literary history.

Youth writing anthologies evince the same power dynamics of editing and publishing that concerned Black Arts literary projects. Writers and artists in and around Black Arts understood "the production—not just the composition"—of literature as central to cultural nationalism, as Howard Rambsy demonstrates.[14] While Black presses such as Detroit's Broadside provided opportunities for creating and circulating literature, many adult writers of the era continued to navigate white-controlled avenues of publication, particularly in New York City, the unofficial capital of white-dominated presses.[15] "The frustration of working thru these bullshit white people shd be obvious," the editors of the groundbreaking Black Arts literary anthology *Black Fire* complained of their press in 1969. Ed Bullins staged related editorial politics in a 1971 short play dramatizing a Black writer's rejection of a white professor's invitation for inclusion in an anthology of "Radical/Protest/People's Poetry." Only when "our serious black artists . . . edit anthologies themselves," Addison Gayle argued in 1971, would "the present renaissance in black letters . . . escape the fate of its predecessor in the nineteen twenties, and endure. Then and only then will the revolution in black letters gain viability and continue right on!"[16] In the moment of Gayle's writing, youth writing collections were on the rise, with child writers across the country producing and publishing their work, often under white adult supervision and sponsorship. Circa-1970 youth writing demonstrates how self-determination is not an absolute binary—either present or absent—but rather an experimental and ongoing process, a locus of diverse strategies that productively complicate cultural politics and open space for fresh forms of expression. Black Arts–era children and adults together treated literary production as a laboratory for dreams and tactics of freedom.

In conversation with Black Arts adults, circa-1970 Black and Puerto Rican child authors creatively used their constraints to shape questions about the nature of personal and artistic agency. As they contested racist forms of white control, young writers also dreamed up their own potential to make change, connect to the people around them, and live freely. This opening of the imaginative space of freedom resonates with recent treatments of Black Arts–era aesthetics. I find that circa-1970 young writers practice what Margo Natalie Crawford terms "black anticipatory aesthetics," a form of futurity that gestures toward and makes room for what is not yet present. "When the BAM mobilized the word 'black' in the most radical manner, it was a way of naming the unknown dimensions of freedom and self-determination," Crawford argues.[17] Black Arts work evokes expressive and political possibilities beyond the literal content of the movement's statements and representations. The anticipatory orientation of Black Arts unfolded in part through engagements with childhood, as adults of the movement created children's books and programs that encouraged young people to embrace Black identity, culture, and language. These texts, Katharine Capshaw argues, conceived of childhood as a "liberatory process" that "embodied both a nationalist ideal and its incomplete fruition"—a characterization that resonates with Crawford's emphasis on the unknown and unrealized.[18] Building on Capshaw's analysis of portrayals of Black childhood in largely adult-authored texts, I assert children's active, self-conscious role in authoring this "liberatory process."

Recognizing children's role in Black Arts reflects the movement's own interest in deconstructing hierarchies of cultural production and consumption, including those based on age. David Grundy observes that both the Black Arts Movement and its predecessor Umbra, a 1960s Lower East Side collective of Black poets, "refused distinctions of age and prestige," pointedly publishing well-known writers next to "complete unknowns," many of whom were barely out of youth themselves.[19] It is fitting, then, to find that many Umbra and Black Arts poets of New York City actively supported and collaborated with child authors. In turn, Black and Puerto Rican young New Yorkers brought an age-specific perspective to the era's literary production. Not only their developmental stage but also their entanglement within public schools, prisons, and other institutional structures defined their youthful status and brought urgency to their interrogations of the present and imaginings of the future. Through this work, young writers intervened in cultural debates about freedom and voice. Children wrote themselves into the apparently adult literary projects around them, even while authoring a distinctively youthful literary movement of their own.

CHILD AUTHORS IN ANTI-RACIST CHILDREN'S LITERATURE

The Black Arts Movement helped galvanize new stories and styles in literature for children. As many adult Black Arts authors wrote children's books, so did young authors of the era write for both adult and child readerships. Circa-1970 young writers are little-recognized contributors to the radical reshaping of children's literature in the era. Recognizing children's own contributions to children's literature yields lessons for scholarship in the twenty-first century. Specifically, the story of circa-1970 youth writing demonstrates the link between two apparently unconnected currents in children's literary studies today: the turn to child agency and the continuing drive to dismantle white supremacy in the field.

Recent scholarship in children's literature considers the role of actual children as writers and active readers, against the convention of solely analyzing adult-authored works for hypothetical child audiences.[20] Fresh conceptualizations of young people's agency break down the boundaries between the academic domains of children's literature studies, childhood studies, and literary studies of childhood, increasingly recognizing the entanglements of texts "by, for and about children," in Rachel Conrad's phrase.[21] This "child agency turn" has coincided with a period of transformative anti-racist work in both the children's literature industry and the academy. Historically, dominant spaces of children's literary studies undermined Black studies and ethnic studies. Marilisa Jiménez García argues that this exclusion was critical to the formation of children's literature as an academic field. Facing skepticism from adult-focused scholars, academic children's literature studies performed legitimacy and gained entrance to the humanities by canonizing white children's culture, permitting anti-Blackness, and suppressing the lessons of ethnic studies. The resulting discipline largely obscured the history of anti-racist and anti-colonial work in children's literature and culture.[22] Recent research by Jiménez García, Conrad, Capshaw, Nazera Sadiq Wright, and others has illuminated how twentieth-century Puerto Rican and African American intellectuals and activists, particularly women, shaped interconnected practices of children's culture and anti-racist, anti-colonial organizing.[23] I trace this genealogy into the work of young people themselves, revealing how children's own literary practices challenged white supremacist forms and shaped new political possibilities in children's literature and culture.

While scholarly commitments to child agency and to racial justice are often framed separately, youth writing reveals their deep connections. When young people like Elisa investigate their own authorship, they are also sharpening our attention to the ways in which reading and writing take shape in the context of white supremacy and other power structures. "Since questions of youth agency are ultimately questions of justice," Conrad argues, cases of adult-supported youth writing "also afford attention to how young poets represent age-based and racial injustice."[24] In both these arenas, young writers push us to ask: whose voices are heard in America?

Child authorship has historically played a role in anti-racist movements. The early 1920s African American children's magazine *The Brownies' Book*, a spin-off of the NAACP's *The Crisis*, featured children's own creative writings and letters to the editors.[25] Decades later, civil rights activists brought youth

writing into the Freedom Schools, the radical education project organized by
the Student Nonviolent Coordinating Committee (SNCC) during Freedom
Summer in Mississippi in 1964. In a key precedent to youth anthologies of the
later 1960s, SNCC published *Freedom School Poetry, a collection* authored by
students of all ages, with a cover illustration by eleven-year-old Larry Martin
and a foreword by Langston Hughes.[26] Apparently singular documents like
The Brownies' Book and *Freedom School Poetry* invite us to imagine the possible
scope of historical African American children's and other young people's literacy practices beyond the extant archive. Youth writing in circa-1970 New York
City is surely one of many understudied literary movements that have been
shaped by marginalized young people and have advanced anti-racist projects.

Circa-1970 children's culture specifically offers evidence for the link
between commitments to youth agency and racial justice. I find it no coinci-
dence that young authors' rise to prominence coincided with a flourishing of
Black, multicultural, and anti-racist adult-authored children's literature in the
late 1960s and early 1970s. Picture books such as John Steptoe's *Stevie* (1969)
and young adult novels such as Virginia Hamilton's *The Planet of Junior Brown*
(1971) portrayed a New York City defined by the lives and imaginations of
Black children.[27]

Youth voice pervades children's books of the era in underrecognized ways,
as adults joined with young people to dismantle the white supremacy and
colonialism of children's culture and imagine new possibilities for the field.
This underrecognized collaboration is exemplified in the biographies of two
prominent adults. First, June Jordan nurtured the youth writing collective
the Voice of the Children, which I explore in chapter 1, as she was launching
her own career as a published author. Jordan brought the lives and voices
of her young collaborators into her works for child readers, particularly
the 1969 picture book *Who Look at Me* and the 1971 young adult novel *His
Own Where.* Jordan's papers show that she based the two heroes of *His Own
Where* on members of the Voice of the Children. Sometimes credited as
the first novel written entirely in Black English, *His Own Where* develops
its poetic prose and radical vision of youth activism in conversation with
Jordan's young poetic collaborators.[28] Meanwhile, education scholar Nancy
Larrick increasingly incorporated youth writing into her study of children's
literature. Larrick's oft-cited 1965 essay "The All-White World of Children's
Books" opens by quoting a five-year-old's own words about children's book
characters: "Why are they always *white* children?" Larrick continues, "With

a child's uncanny wisdom, she [the quoted five-year-old] singled out one of the most critical issues in American education today: the almost complete omission of Negroes from books for children."[29] Although the essay does not explicitly discuss youth authorship, Larrick responded to her own call to transform children's literature by spending much of the next decade printing and promoting young people's writing. She published anthologies of child writers and wrote articles, edited collections, and organized conferences on the topic.[30] Larrick's career choices suggest that she, like Jordan, understood young writers as critical to the project of racial justice. Such leading adult thinkers have turned to young people themselves for guidance in challenging white supremacy and thinking critically about the concepts of diversity and voice in children's culture.

CHILD AUTHORS IN 1960S–1970S CULTURE: POLITICS, EDUCATION, AND POETICS

The examples of June Jordan and Nancy Larrick point to young authors' political and cultural force in circa-1970 New York City and the U.S. at large. Youth writing mattered to audiences of all ages in this era, finding resonance with a range of political positions and agendas. The circa-1970 case demonstrates how youth writing can extend influence across a broad swath of cultural concerns. In the post–civil rights years, child authorship operated politically, pedagogically, and poetically: both drawing on and helping shape ideas in politics; in education; and in language, literature, and the arts.

Politically, children were fitting authorities for a moment when U.S. culture was rethinking the idea of authority itself. Disillusion with urban renewal and the War on Poverty, the 1968 assassination of Martin Luther King, Jr., the breakup of the civil rights coalition, and the escalation of the Vietnam War, among other events, increased distrust in government, media, and mainstream institutions as sources of truth and drivers of social change. Radical political and cultural projects, such as the Black Arts Movement, the Puerto Rican Movement, the Chicano Movement, and the American Indian Movement, asserted conceptions of truth, cultural value, and justice outside of white Western norms. In this moment of deep change, circa-1970 youth writing assumed the moral authority carried by childhood in the 1950s–1960s civil rights movement. Quintessentially minor by way of both age and race, Black and Puerto Rican children appeared to both liberal and radical adults as "raw," bracingly honest voices of truth and models of the "sheer tenacity of the human spirit against oppression."[31] The old notion of children's laudable freshness to the world took new political form in the idea that the young remained relatively untainted by the corrupt, deadening flow of white Western norms. Paradoxically, the same youth writing anthologies that could be read as irredeemably compromised by white adult intervention drew their appeal partly from their apparent immunity to compromise.

Young writers themselves both interrogated and accepted their moral mantle. Although the image of marginalized children's truthful purity sometimes indulged cliché or even fetish, child writers also took advantage of this image by presenting themselves as distinctively qualified to speak truth about American society. Sixth-grader Luis, a schoolmate of Carmen and Elisa, puts his exceptional position as a child to work in a passage both wistful and forceful. Luis declares: "A wish I want is so beautiful that you might not understand it. . . . I have always said that I wished that all wars, riots, killings and prejudice would stop." The trope of a child's sweet wishing frames a popular sentiment voiced by many child writers and other Americans of the era: the urgent dream of an end to racism and violence. This image of wishing takes on a firmer edge with Luis's claim to long-held beliefs: "I have always said . . ." Luis recruits his childhood status once more to conclude his discussion on no uncertain terms: "So if it comes from a boy living in a slum in the Lower East Side, Listen baby, if you don't 'STOP IT' you people are going to get it man and I say get it, get it."[32] Luis calls attention to his own marginalized class, age, and neighborhood identity. From this position, he can not only speak with the authority of experience but also potentially reach readers who will be receptive to such a revolutionary message only "if it comes from a boy living in a slum." At the same time, the conditional *if* casts doubt on this framing. Self-presenting as a boy in a slum may be a useful political tactic, but it falls short of the speaker's full subjectivity. Luis's writing both cries out for peace and, on another level, uses that cry as the occasion to investigate his own writerly positionality and authority.

Taking my cue from young writers like Luis, I both dissect idealizations of child voice and proceed on the premise that circa-1970 young writers were doing something special. As residents of oppressed neighborhoods and attendees of a largely failing public educational system, who were frequently invoked in political discourse and targeted by policing but also active in liberation movements, Black and Puerto Rican children commanded a clear vantage on New York City after civil rights. Young writers' small-scale acts of positioning model the challenge of navigating the promises and perils of the post–civil rights US, as the nation simultaneously sought out narratives of antiracism and social critique and rolled out new technologies of racist violence and deprivation. In this way, children built a literary movement equipped to confront the circa-1970 moment of both radical anti-racist possibility and War on Crime racial order.

In education, youth writing served partly as a site of experimentation and radical reimagining of American schooling after civil rights. The collapse of desegregation ambitions in the 1960s left school inequities untouched even while dismantling community-based structures of Black pedagogy that had been built outside of white view during legal segregation.[33] The extremities of racist deprivation and violence in schools serving Black and Latinx children created a "height of discontent with American educational institutions" at the close of the 1960s.[34] It is difficult to overstate the school system's failure to serve Puerto Rican children in New York and other US mainland cities. Academic and institutional studies sometimes brought insight but also frequently pathologized families experiencing poverty and racism. Throughout the 1960s, Puerto Ricans, organized studies, conferences, and activist organizations—some including youth membership—to challenge the "catastrophic" dropout rate and test scores, the use of textbooks and popular children's books rife with racist stereotypes, and the lack of bilingual and culturally respectful curricula, as well as to imagine and propose new approaches to schooling for mainland Puerto Rican children, particularly in New York.[35] Local coalitions also drew on newly available federal Head Start funding to form experimental, neighborhood-centric early childhood education programs.[36] Children's literacy thus held center stage in anti-racist and anti-colonial movements.

Young writers of circa-1970 New York were at the center of a nationally important struggle for anti-racist schooling. In the community control movement of the late 1960s, Black and Puerto Rican families, educators, and community leaders in the city collaboratively envisioned and briefly piloted public schools almost entirely directed by neighborhood residents in specific experimental districts, most famously Brooklyn's Ocean Hill–Brownsville neighborhood. The experimental districts were shut down, however, after the city's United Federation of Teachers went on strike to protest community-controlled schools' attempts to transfer out some teachers and administrators. The strike shut down nine hundred schools for two months, leaving

1.1 million students out of class, and prompted virulently racialized media coverage across the U. S. The rise and fall of community control powerfully affected not only public education but also beliefs about self-determination, interracial relations, and the politics of bureaucracy in the city at large.[37]

Youth writing programs were shaped by educational activism in New York, and published children's writings were received in part as dispatches from this struggle. Children in community-controlled schools wrote poetry in and out of class. During the United Federation of Teachers strike, a reading of poetry by Ocean Hill–Brownsville students on the radio sparked national attention.[38] Students formed publications such as *What's Happening*, a literary magazine that circulated at schools across the city.[39] Outside of the public school system, a flourishing of Pan-African nationalist independent schools, experimental "storefront" schools, and informal learning collectives emphasized youth voice and political consciousness, as Russell Rickford demonstrates.[40] Even when youth writing production was based in public school classrooms and other institutional spaces, it drew on the pedagogical and political thought of these alternative sites of schooling.

Schoolchildren's own political activity informed their creative work. While the late 1960s and early 1970s are often associated with college student activism, junior high and high school students across New York City were conducting their own campaigns for change in their schools. Young New Yorkers worked for bilingual education, Black studies curricula, improved support for Black and Latinx students, and an end to strictures like dress codes.[41] Children organized in and out of schools and crafted their own terms for racial justice, often closely tied to opposition to the Vietnam War. A school official dubbed one Brooklyn high school "Mayor Lindsay's Vietnam"—a label that suggests the tone of the city's response to troublemaking activism.[42] Young people's political actions operated both with and without adult support, always in conversation with contemporaneous adult movements but also distinct from them. Through literary production, young people prepared for, remembered, examined, and shared their political experiences. If, as James Smethurst argues, the Black Arts Movement was the "cultural wing" of the Black Power Movement and Black Power was the "political wing" of Black Arts, youth writing can be understood as a cultural counterpart to the political work of 1960s–1970s young people.[43]

Grassroots currents in education coincided with a wave of investment from government and academic institutions targeted at teaching creativity to American students. In the decade after Sputnik, funding flowed in accordance with anxieties about the US education system's preparation of the next generation. English educators argued that their discipline was as urgent to the moment as math and science, as demonstrated by the grave title of a 1961 report of the National Council of Teachers of English, *The National Interest and the Teaching of English*. In a series of conferences and curricular development efforts, mostly famously the 1966 Dartmouth Seminar, English educators debated strategies for engaging students outside the stale textbook conventions of rigid language rules and memorization.[44] In student writing, as in science laboratories, children's creativity and inventiveness were imagined as drawing a contrast with Soviet authoritarianism and showcasing the rewards of American democracy.[45] Meanwhile, the postwar prominence of psychoanalysis and psychology inspired belief in writing's therapeutic value and capacity to tap into hidden dimensions of thought and feeling. Writing would promote Cold War social order by encouraging psychological development, releasing tensions, and facilitating the adjustment of the inner life to the social world.[46] Child authorship thus held promise for radical and liberal agendas alike.

Youth writing provided a site for educators and for Americans at large to reckon with the state of education after civil rights. In a late 1960s wave of school muckraking books, teachers took note of the contrast between pedagogical declarations in the amply funded halls of Dartmouth and the everyday realities of city classrooms that were literally falling apart, held few or no reading materials and supplies, and received often laughable administrative oversight.[47] These teacher accounts often incorporated writings by students as a coup de grace against the school system and a reminder of its stakes. Creative writing found fertile ground in the classrooms of poor and working-class students in part because these children's classrooms were the least protected, leaving some teachers with little training and plenty of pedagogical freedom. In the preface to one popular anthology, teacher-editor Irving Benig explains that he came to his Brooklyn classroom through a program that allowed young men to avoid the military draft by teaching in an underserved city school.[48] The majority of teachers who compiled circa-1970 youth anthologies considered themselves agents of resistance within a racist and corrupt school system. These teacher-editors sought not only to share students' insights but also to inspire outrage and educational reform.

Youth anthologies, which were sometimes federally funded or school-published yet frequently compiled in some degree of antiestablishment spirit, straddled often-clashing institutional and grassroots approaches to education. Even as adult leaders of radical movements cultivated and circulated children's writings, the same texts appealed to readers who were not necessarily receptive to the messages of, for instance, the Black Panther Party. Children offered an apparently nonthreatening form of reckoning with the failures of social change. For instance, Luis's warning "you people are going to get it" is softened by his self-professed status as a child, as Luis himself would know well. Engaging both radical and liberal readerships, circa-1970 youth writing demonstrates how the cultural category of childhood brings together disparate politics and belief systems in ways that can both fuel and dispel drives for social change.

Even outside of school settings, adult writers and thinkers were drawn to the sounds and styles of circa-1970 child writers as a source of fresh poetics. Adults of the 1960s and 1970s often perceived youth writing to have a distinct character that touched central concerns and hopes about American language. At the risk of stereotyping both children's work and the adult literary movements around it, considering the era's poetry in broad strokes reveals a striking resonance with children's writing.

Children's reputation for freshness and honesty promised to advance an aim pursued by diverse groups, including Black Arts, the developing Nuyorican Poetry movement, the New York School, and feminist poets: the search for literary forms that could break the hold of ossified Western conventions and enact energetic transformations of language and art. Phillip Lopate, an essential chronicler of youth writing pedagogy, notes that at a time when "the newspaper carried Pentagon neologisms and euphemisms such as 'pacification,'" youth writing advocates saw literacy education as a way to rescue language.[49] New York School poets sought to disrupt stale Western traditions with humor, playful wordings, and language games—forms proximal to children's culture. Black Arts writers, meanwhile, challenged the primacy of White Mainstream English and centered the histories, linguistic structures, and expressive possibilities of Black English. Black Arts poets "frequently repudiated standard modes of capitalization, spelling, punctuation, and syntax in favor of typography and orthography meant to represent a written vernacular speech and other sonic forms of black culture," Evie Shockley notes.[50] In line with this project, children's writings frequently deviated from conventional spelling, grammar, and orthography. These departures could be inadvertent—the result of children's tactics such as sounding out spellings—or represent matters of taste—for instance, using inconsistent

verb tense to play with time or emphasizing a statement with four exclama-
tion points in a row.[51] Children used these forms whether working in Black
English, White Mainstream English, or other vernacular forms.[52] The era's
challenge to textual convention heightened interest in young people's perceived proximity to orality, since children generally speak before writing and
frequently think and read out loud.

Hitched to specific moments of time and age, children's texts conjured an
air of immediacy in line with Black Arts and Puerto Rican cultural invest-
ments in liveness, performance, and ephemerality. The brevity of most children's texts suited them for performance, circulation, and anthologization,
the preferred methods of 1960s literary exchange. Anthologies—along with
journals and magazines, which young writers of the era also produced—
pooled money and other resources in a structurally racist book industry and
strengthened minority literary networks. Emphasizing multivocality and
mixing genres, collections such as *Black Fire* and Miguel Algarín and Miguel
Piñero's 1975 volume *Nuyorican Poetry* mapped the diversity as well as the
collective terms and values within each developing literary movement.[53] Like
their adult counterparts, marginalized child writers used anthologies to build
and claim a groundbreaking literary project, even when those volumes were
edited and controlled by white adults. No wonder that leading figures of Black
Arts, Puerto Rican/ Nuyorican poetry, the New York School, and other literary movements frequently worked with child writers. Youth writing created
a generative occasion for writers of all ages to examine ideas about language.

CHILD AUTHORS IN THE NEW YORK LITERARY SCENE

Despite young authors' potent influence, accounts of the 1960s New York
cultural scene rarely consider children's place in it. Sparsely documented,
the place of ordinary children emerges through a "weak theory" lens of
small anecdotes, social ties, proximities, and speculations.[54] The following
vignettes surface signs of children's role in the city's literary milieu. By claiming children's place in the circa-1970 New York scene, I aim to demonstrate
the value of my narrow temporal and regional focus, which matches previous
full-length studies of short-lived but influential poetic projects among adults.
Concentrated attention to the stories and styles of such projects reveals their
strategies, underlying philosophies, and lasting impact—while also bringing
poetic pasts to life for readers in the present.[55]

Children touched one of the most iconic sites of the 1960s countercultural scene, St. Mark's Church in-the-Bowery , a Lower East Side church with a history of supporting radical arts. In 1966, St. Mark's launched the Poetry Project, a celebrated site for readings, workshops, the nurturing of early-career poets, and the development of radical literary styles. In his study of the 1960s Lower East Side poetry scene, Daniel Kane reports that the Poetry Project thrived in part due to securing "nearly $200,000 in federal government money earmarked for the socialization of juvenile delinquents." With the help of a New School sociologist, St. Mark's Church applied to the federal Health, Education, and Welfare Office of Juvenile Delinquency and Development for a grant in "Creative Arts for Alienated Youth." The church and its partners had no intention of conducting children's programs. By invoking "disaffected youth," the grant application intentionally conflated the mostly white, early-career poets of middle-class background on the Lower East Side scene with the actual children of the neighborhood, who were primarily Latinx, Black, and Asian American. The mixture of white suspicion and sympathy directed at these children was so potent that a mere invocation of deviant youth could release a wave of government funds. This anecdote functions in Kane's adult-focused narrative as a moment of ethically questionable writerly mischief, one that succeeded at the expense of the neighborhood's ostensibly "silent though real impoverished youth."[56] The Lower East Side's young people, however, were far from "silent." Though not the true target of the Poetry Project's fundraising, children nevertheless made their presence and their poetry known in and around St. Mark's. Several members of the youth writing collective the Voice of the Children were on their way to June Jordan and Clarence Major's joint reading at St. Mark's on April 4, 1968, when the news came that Martin Luther King, Jr., had been shot. Jordan and Major decided to continue with the reading, and child and adult writers experienced April 4 in the space together. Several children worked on their own poetry during the reading; a work by one child, Michael Goode, would appear the following week in the *Village Voice*, as I will discuss in chapter 1.[57] In 1970, the Voice of the Children would conduct their own poetry reading at St. Mark's, demonstrating young writers' artistically active, socially embedded position in the neighborhood.[58]

The Lower East Side's "low-rent cosmopolitanism" was the world not only of John Ashbery and Amiri Baraka but also of Elisa and her friends.[59] These apparently separate societies—that of hip and famous men out on the town and that of schoolgirls writing and laughing on a tenement floor—were in fact interwoven. Carmen and Elisa's work circulated widely in the bestselling anthology *Can't You Hear Me Talking to You?* Lower East Side legends such as Denise Levertov and Ron Padgett worked extensively with child writers in public school classrooms.[60] Leading New York School poet Kenneth Koch dedicated much of his career to reading and writing poetry with children, while Black Mountain and New York School poet Joel Oppenheimer was not only the director of the St. Mark's Poetry Project but also the 1968–69 director of the youth writing initiative Teachers & Writers Collaborative (T&W). Given Oppenheimer's tendency to do all administrative business for T&W in the storied Lion's Head pub in Greenwich Village, one can imagine discussions of children's writing pervading even the most adult space of countercultural bars.[61]

As the late 1960s rise of the Black Arts Movement galvanized cultural activity throughout New York City, children participated in literary networks across the boroughs. As Capshaw documents, celebrated child poet Kali Grosvenor associated with the most celebrated echelon of Black Arts figures—joining Black Arts poet Sonia Sanchez and South African exiled activist and poet Keorapetse Kgositsile (Bra Willie) onstage and reportedly befriending "'Auntie Nina' (Simone)" and "'Auntie Maya' (Angelou)."[62] Though Grosvenor was publicized as an exceptional "superkid," thanks in part to her mother's stature, less famous children practiced their own versions of productivity and sociality in the Black Arts scene.[63] For instance, Sonia Sanchez not only collaborated with Grosvenor but also worked with child writers through T&W, which facilitated creative writing programming in low-income neighborhood schools across the city.

Young T&W collaborators Alvin Curry and Robert Jackson demonstrate the breadth of ordinary children's literary activity. As former students of Herbert Kohl, who launched T&W in 1967, Alvin Curry and Jackson helped shape the new organization.[64] Alvin Curry provided feedback on the manuscript of Kohl's successful memoir-cum-anthology *36 Children*, which recounts how his and Jackson's sixth-grade Harlem class shaped Kohl's philosophies of pedagogy and of writing. In the first years of T&W, visitors would frequently encounter office regulars Jackson and Alvin, then in their midteens. The pair likely engaged with rising stars active with T&W, such

as Anne Sexton, Larry Neal, and Muriel Rukeyser, as well as the organization's prominent supporters, including Academy of American Poets director Elizabeth Kray and *New York Review of Books* editor Robert Silvers.[65]
According to one T&W employee's recollections, Alvin and Jackson spent
many hours in the office with David Henderson, an Umbra poet who taught
for T&W and came to the office regularly.[66] Other regulars included photographer and filmmaker James Hinton as well as Victor Hernández Cruz,
who was just out of high school himself, a younger member of Umbra and a
fast-rising poetry star. Housed at Horace Mann School in the Bronx, T&W
shared office space with local members of the SNCC, a key mover in the
civil rights movement, and with the nationally known youth writing collective What's Happening.[67] The name "What's Happening" aptly describes
the milieu of youth writing in the late 1960s. Through their creative work
and their physical presence, Alvin Curry and Robert Jackson helped shape a
"happening" hub of cultural and political action. Apparently ordinary children lived and worked among celebrated, artistically and politically groundbreaking adults, as youth writing touched diverse nodes of the 1960s scene.

Alvin Curry and Robert Jackson represent their position in their creative
works. Jackson, a talented artist, designed the first issue of the T&W newsletter, a still-running publication featuring children's work and adults' reflections on teaching. Jackson's title page for this first issue features a black ink
line drawing of Alvin Curry churning out stories at a typewriter, under the
grand label "The Man of Many Fables" (fig. 1). Fables were a T&W teaching
fad, and Alvin did indeed write many of them, which appeared in the T&W
newsletter and in Kohl's book *36 Children*. But Jackson portrays Alvin outside of the bounds of school and childhood norms. He is a working writer,
stylishly dressed, with sunglasses and a cigarette dangling from his lips. He
plugs away at a typewriter—a device and skill inaccessible to most children
of the era.[68] Particularly in light of the close association of fables with childhood, the title and image of "The Man of Many Fables" engage ironically with
the cultural construction of the hip writer as an adult, specifically a man. As
a teenager, Alvin might make a claim to manhood, but as a T&W mainstay
and fable writer, his access to publication was premised on his proximity to
childhood. Both teasing and championing his friend, Jackson claims Alvin's
place among adult working artists like Henderson. Jackson, like Elisa, art-
fully portrays a friend's artmaking in a testament to their generation's creative
production.

FIGURE 1. Robert G. Jackson, "Alvin Curry: The Man of Many Fables." Cover of *Teachers and Writers Collaborative Newsletter* 1, no. 1 (September 1967). —Courtesy of Teachers & Writers Collaborative.

Children were an integral part of what James Smethurst calls the "word-of-mouth (or text) network" of Black Arts in New York, the social system that nourished cultural production and exchange outside of white-dominated gate-keeping structures.[69] Children moved fluidly among institutional and informal spaces, written and oral forms, private and public artistic venues. Young people not only socialized with adults but also helped structure the sociality of literature in the era. "Historians like to fix and x-ray avant-garde movements and analyze them in terms of process or product," Lorenzo Thomas argues in his study of African American poets on the 1960s Lower East Side. "Those who find themselves attracted to such vortices, however, know that the avant-garde is less about change in the arts than it is about genuine experimentation in social relations."[70] Thomas emphasizes not only the social nature of artistic movements but also the dynamic, unstable, and nuanced quality of that sociality. Ties between children and adults, I propose, have served as a key site for this experimentation, as writers invented forms of artistic collaboration, solidarity, and nationalism and tested out their respective risks, possibilities, and creative consequences.

IDENTITY TERMS AND CATEGORIES

The study of youth writing requires naming and defining marginalized young people despite my incomplete knowledge of them. Anthology editors of the 1960s and 1970s often referred to their young contributors as "Black and Puerto Rican." While the youth literary movement examined here is indeed distinctly Black and Puerto Rican as well as rooted in working-class and poor neighborhoods, individual writers' racial, ethnic, and class identities are often unclear. Youth writing anthologies provide little information about their contributors, and children were often credited under pseudonyms, first names, or initials. Through the imperfect category *Black and Puerto Rican youth writing*, I intend to hold room for a range of identities—sometimes intersectional and overlapping—from which children may have written. My use of the term *Black* denotes a range of African Diasporic identities with attention to young writers' close connections to the Black Power, Black Arts, and Black English movements. In addition to discussing *Puerto Rican* young writers, I use the term *Latinx* when specific heritage is unclear, as well as when discussing events relevant to multiple Latinx identities. While Puerto Rican art and experience specifically are central to circa-1970 youth writing in New York, Dominican and other young New Yorkers may have made unacknowledged contributions to the literature discussed here. My readings have developed largely through the theoretical and methodological frameworks of Black studies, including scholarship on the multiethnic diversity and Afro-Latinx currents within the Black Arts Movement. Much work remains to understand Puerto Rican and other Latinx young writers' works and experiences in the era.

Age raises additional questions of terminology. I examine authors between the ages of nine and eighteen. I include authors' ages or school grades when available. While age labels may color our readings of texts—after all, adults' ages are rarely in their bylines—age fundamentally shapes these authors' experiences of and approaches to public writing.[71] Age also structures children's schooling, family relations, access to politics and culture, and vulnerability to racism. Retaining age markers may thus sharpen attention to each writer's social position and relationship to the category of childhood. I intentionally use the terms *child*, *youth*, and *young person* interchangeably.

Writers of the era claimed their membership in the category of "children's voices" into their mid-to-late teenage years. *Youth* was and remains a loaded term. It evokes the war declared by President John F. Kennedy and waged by subsequent administrations against "juvenile delinquency and youth crime," the specter of non-white young people out of order that, as Elizabeth Hinton has established, was essential to the buildup of mass policing and incarceration.[72] The semantic division between *childhood* and *youth* may conspire in the eviction of Black and Latinx young people from the category of childhood.[73] But *youth* has also become a term of empowerment, as well as a critique of white supremacy's tight grip on the category of *childhood*.[74] By using the term *youth* together with *children* and *young writers*, I intend to keep these histories in mind while also foregrounding writers' own relationships to age.

While centering young writers, I also tell the stories of children's older collaborators. I examine how adults, who often did not share children's racial, ethnic, and class identities, variously supported and betrayed children's free expression and public reception—stories that certainly hold lessons for my own scholarship. In the twenty-first-century moment of reckoning with white supremacy and reimagining the terms of #OwnVoices and #Other-Voices practices, the messy, sometimes painful history of child-adult creative collaborations offers both cautionary tales and testaments to the potential of clumsy and imperfect attempts to work with and relate to others across differences of power.[75]

I write as a student of 1960s–1970s child authors, who themselves spur us to reexamine our ideas about categories of race, ethnicity, class, gender, and age. In her discussion of identity terms, historian Tiya Miles provides a motto that children and adults alike might echo: "I am practicing at my letters."[76]

CHAPTER OUTLINE

The first three chapters of *Writing Themselves into the Movement* trace the conceptual and stylistic contours of Black and Puerto Rican youth writing in late 1960s and early 1970s New York City. Each of these chapters identifies a rhetorical maneuver with which writers interrogate their position as authors and as children in an unfree society. Specifically, circa-1970 young writers deploy unstable forms of second-person address, age-specific forms of anti-racist temporality, and a trope of haunting absence. This set of maneuvers collectively scrutinizes children's authorial circumstances, unsettles white liberal modes of consuming difference, probes the paradox of simultaneous cultural influence and material oppression, and makes space for writers' own imaginative self-inquiries. The interweaving of these tactics across neighborhoods, programs, and individual young authors demonstrates that circa-1970 Black and Puerto Rican young New Yorkers both participated in adult-associated movements of the day and constituted a literary movement of their own.

Chapter 1 examines the Voice of the Children, a Brooklyn-based youth poetry collective founded partly through the efforts of Alvin Curry's sisters, Linda and Pat, and directed by June Jordan and teacher Terri Bush. Building on theorizations of direct address in Black poetics, I argue that young writers use unexpected and unstable forms of the second-person *you* not only to manage readership but also to behold their own poetic selves. Through manipulations of second-person address, the Voice of the Children advances a critique of visibility politics amid proliferating forms of surveillance over Black and Puerto Rican young people.

Turning to school-based writing, chapter 2 argues that classroom authors craft an age-specific approach to the racial politics of time. In the name of exposing educational neglect in de facto segregated schools, the white teacher-editors of two classroom writing anthologies portray their students as imminently doomed. Children themselves contest this narrative of a doomed future with their own temporal terms in classroom writings ranging from dramatic scripts to notes passed between desks. Young writers craft preemptive rhetorical forms that contest the apparently airtight temporal logics used to discipline and pathologize Black and Latinx youth and advance imaginatively disruptive and nonlinear alternatives for understanding time.

Chapter 3 identifies young writers' agency in absentia, or creative influence exerted at a distance. Specifically, young writers use a trope of haunting absence to probe the divergence between the increasing policing and containment of their bodies in the physical space of New York City and the mobility of their highly popular writings as they circulated through US culture. I trace this dynamic within *The Me Nobody Knows*, a 1970 Broadway hit with lyrics pulled almost entirely from the writings of Black and Puerto Rican boys, some of whom wrote while incarcerated. In letters, fables, and sci-fi tales adapted for the musical stage, children's deployments of haunting absence presciently extend their influence to Broadway while registering the increasing constraints on boys' bodies at the dawn of the War on Crime.

I turn from literary production to reception in chapter 4, which critiques adults' typical interpretations of youth writing, yielding lessons for readers today. Undermining the literary validity of children's writing even in apparent acclaim, reviewers set up the genre to fall into obscurity—a pattern that young people of the time perceived and challenged. I explore young people's reception of their own reception as well as an alternative critical approach to youth writing developed by June Jordan.

Despite failures of critical recognition, young writers of the Black Arts era found surprising ways to extend their influence, continuing to shape cultural concepts of youth voice and anti-racist literature into the twenty-first century. The epilogue visits a twenty-first-century restaging of one circa-1970 poet's verse to examine the persistent influence of the era's youth writing, even as the material conditions of children's lives remain unacceptable. The impact of Black and Puerto Rican young authors over half a century prompts me to reconsider the cultural concept of "listening to the children."

Youth writers of the Black Arts era devise rhetorical means to become theorists of their own authorship and commentators on the very idea of having a voice in New York City and in America. Calling attention to the controls exerted by white adult power structures on youth authorship, children charge their writings with the tensions of these circumstances, making vivid the precarity of young writers' position and the stakes of their words. Children's analyses of their own authorial position serve not only to scrutinize the realities of racism but also to inspect, imagine, and savor fresh possibilities for their own inner lives and collective dreams.

CHAPTER I

Poetic Self-Witness

*Second-Person Plays in
the Voice of the Children*

black child,
step in the back
and just don't be noticed,
for if you do,
you will be bottled
for eternity,
to never be seen again.

Fourteen-year-old Phillip Solomon portrays a double bind of racial surveillance, in line with LeRoi Jones's (Amiri Baraka) description of "the
torture of being the unseen object, and, the constantly observed subject."[1] In
Solomon's untitled poem, reproduced in its entirety in this chapter's epigraph,
a lowercase whisper urges the Black child to evade sight, which could only
bring a deeper and more permanent state of invisibility. Under this delicate
hair-trigger of attention, even a casual glance is dangerous: simply to be
"noticed" dooms the child. The threat of being bottled like soda, presumably
by white adults, portrays violent commodification, as well as hinting at the
literal imprisonment of Black young people who are caught in the notice of
policing structures. Yet the fantastic image of human bottling also conjures a
magic genie or a seaborne message in a bottle, suggesting the child's access to
powerful forms even under constraint. Doubling back on its own paradox, the
poem calls attention to the Black child through the act of urging the opposite.

Published in the bestselling 1971 anthology *The Voice of the Children*, Solomon's poem seems to disregard its own warning. The poet thus displays his ability to navigate the treacherous waters of white adult attention. This maneuver depends on second-person voice. By directing the poem to *you*, Solomon puts the Black child's vulnerability in tension with the poet's capacity for powerful speech. In this sense, Solomon does "step in the back," behind the veil of the second person, disrupting the common tendency to tie children's writing back to the testimony of an autobiographical *I*. Solomon's second-person structure creates ambiguity around the speaker's stance. His verse could be read as an inner dialogue, as a direct warning to peers, as an expression of shared experience among peers, or as an admonishment to white adults. Alternately, the poem could parrot the advice of adults, which the poet has ignored. This plurality unsettles the position of readers, even as the portrayal of the destructive force of attention casts doubt on the act of reading itself.

Solomon's complex approach to audience reflects the conditions of literary production within the Voice of the Children, a nationally recognized youth writing collective that ran in New York City from 1967 to 1971. Codirected by adults June Jordan and Terri Bush for Black and Puerto Rican young people, the group attracted coverage in local and national newspapers and invitations to perform at festivals, on the radio, and on TV. A 1969 *New York Times* article describing a "Renaissance of Black Poets," for example, ended by quoting a short story by fourteen-year-old Voice of the Children member Wayne Figueroa, whose photograph appeared in the article between portraits of adult poets Gylan Kain and Nikki Giovanni.[2] Attention to the group culminated in the 1970 release by Holt, Rinehart and Winston of the group's popular self-titled volume. The Voice of the Children poets knew that their texts were circulating not only among children but also among adults of different races. Adult support could be the mobilizing but constraining bottle that carried children's words across the US, bringing added opportunities to be heard or misconstrued.

As something close to a best-case scenario for anti-racist, sensitive adult collaboration, *The Voice of the Children* has received more scholarly attention than other anthologies of the era. Present-day adults can learn much from this history about supporting young writers, as Rachel Conrad asserts in a key critical treatment of the group. Jordan and Bush are remarkable models for "build[ing] a platform for children to name political realities, assert their perspectives about contemporary concerns, and claim space to critique unjust structures of power."[3] Yet the group's few years of thriving depended on a constant struggle against white adult manipulation, misrepresentation, and commodification of children's work, as well as pragmatic issues, such as a lack of funding. These challenges register in the Voice of the Children's poetics.

Even while skillfully interrogating and managing the interracial and inter-generational conditions of their writing, young writers pursued their own agendas, articulating and reimagining the terms of New York City childhood and American life more broadly in the circa-1970 moment. In particular, the Voice of the Children poets used second-person address simultaneously to manage their audience and to create rhetorical space for poetic speakers' witness of themselves. In the case of Solomon's verse, the potent critique of visibility politics serves not only to chasten readers or to warn peers but also to shape the implicit first-person speaker, who is both evasive and strongly felt. Who is the poet that emerges in the act of calling on *you?* What does it feel like to inhabit the voice that invites, demands, appeals, prophecies?

Solomon and his fellow Voice of the Children writers developed youth-specific forms of what Phillip Brian Harper identifies as Black Arts poets' "insistent use of the second-person pronoun."[4] Through direct address to *you,* Harper argues, poets wrestled with the problem of developing a truly unifying Black nationalism. Whereas poems by Amiri Baraka, Nikki Giovanni, and other movement leaders may appear to be "*heard* by blacks and *over*heard by whites," and thus shaped by *interracial* division, these poems primarily operate as "*heard* directly by whites and *over*heard by blacks," in *intraracial* negotiation.[5] At the heart of Harper's discussion, Kevin Quashie reminds us, is the "conundrum of audience in Black Arts poetry, where the goal of speaking against white violence is conflated with the delicate work of trying to call blackness into formation."[6] Harper and Quashie illuminate how calls to *you* navigate the tensions of speech within the context of US racism to do the work of community, connection, and personhood within Black poetic subjectivities. Not coincidentally, both Harper's and Quashie's analyses draw on the poetry of June Jordan, who cofounded and codirected the Voice of the Children workshop. As this chapter demonstrates, Jordan and the workshop's young writers were engaged in a collective, mutually influential poetic project.

I read the Voice of the Children's poetry within Quashie's conception of the second person as a poetic project of "black aliveness." Calls to *you,* Quashie proposes, operate "not as an encasement of the other where the authority resides with the speaker, but as an occasion to consider the tender becoming of the speaking one, the one who calls the scene into being, the one who yields to the risk and possibility of venturing to say 'you.'"[7] Drawing largely on poetry by Black women of the Voice of the Children's era—including Jordan—Quashie's theory illuminates how Solomon's poetic speaker attains presence in the act of urging absence. Through second-person address, as well as plays with the concept of literary error, Solomon and other child authors bend the tense and risky dynamics of public attention toward the purposes of poetic self-witness: the investigation of their own expressive possibilities.

CREATING A YOUTH WRITING COLLECTIVE

The Voice of the Children took shape through both institutional forces and grassroots endeavors, adult leadership and youth organizing. Attending to this plurality of perspectives demonstrates the messy realities of child-adult collaboration. The group's origin stories, moreover, reveal lines of inspiration, influence, and tension that run through group members' poems.

The organizational, funding-based thread of the story begins with the American Academy of Poets. In 1966, the Academy's executive director, Elizabeth "Betty" Kray, founded the first Poets-in-the-Schools program (various Writers-in-the-Schools programs still exist today). Word began to spread among the city's poets that the Academy had "this grant from the government . . . where they'd give poets $75.00 [per day] to read their own poems and read other people's poems and talk to the kids about it."[8] A year later, both building on and rebelling against federally funded initiatives in English education, the educator and writer Herbert Kohl founded the organization Teachers & Writers Collaborative (known as T&W or the Collaborative), which provided resources for professional poets to teach long-term creative writing workshops both in and out of schools.

Here, the institutional story intersects with existing community-based activity. In the autumn of 1967, Kray connected Kohl to writer Ishmael Reed, who introduced Kohl to young poet Victor Hernández Cruz. Cruz and Reed were both active in Umbra, a Lower East Side collective of Black poets that was a predecessor to the Black Arts Movement. Then entering his senior year of high school, Cruz had already published a chapbook and begun his first full-length poetry collection, which would be published by

Random House to acclaim. Through Kohl, Cruz met June Jordan (then June Meyer), an early-career poet, journalist, and activist on the roster of Kray's Poets-in-the-Schools program. Jordan was researching an article for the *Urban Review* about students at East Harlem's notoriously neglectful Benjamin Franklin High School. Jordan interviewed two high-achieving, academic-track students at the school, as well as two students slated to the nonacademic "general" track. The latter pair of students were Cruz and his friend Paul Luciano, the younger brother of Young Lords leader, poet, and soon-to-be T&W member Felipe Luciano. Jordan portrays this pair on the "general" track as creatively and socially awake, while the "academic" students seemed to be lost souls. She quotes Cruz on his plans after graduating high school: "I'm going to go on as a poet. I want to be in that situation where I both write and help people. (He thought for a while and then said:) I want to teach.... Teach whatever I know. Help people by teaching."[9] Cruz's concept of teaching was not confined to classrooms; he was already doing community-based, noninstitutional education and cultural work. Bridging his childhood and adulthood as well as the vocations of writing and teaching, Cruz's words provide a framework for what would become the Voice of the Children. Jordan's *Urban Review* story, meanwhile, reminds us to attend to "undercommons" forms of intellectual, cultural, and social activity, operating under the radar of institutional power.[10]

Cruz and Jordan soon partnered to form a creative writing workshop for young people on Saturday mornings in Harlem, sponsored by T&W. Kohl later said that after reading her *Urban Review* article, he was determined to recruit Jordan for a new writing group, but Jordan's writings suggest that she was largely inspired by Cruz, as well as her own long-developing ideas about childhood.[11] Perhaps Jordan and Cruz recruited T&W as much as it recruited them.

As institutional and grassroots forces intersected, so did the agencies of both adults and children. Kohl's recounting of the Voice of the Children's founding reveals young people's central role: "You know how she [June Jordan] got her students? I told Alvin Curry's sister Linda, 'Linda, you've been bugging me for a while to help you do some writing. But you don't want to get in Alvin's shadow. So why don't you come and bring a bunch of friends?' And she did, and some of the kids brought their teacher at the time, who was Terri Bush. That's how that thing got started ... we nurtured that whole thing."[12] Kohl uses his origin story to take credit for the Voice of the

Children, although it was funded by T&W only initially and garnered public recognition mostly as an independent program. Kohl, a white man, risks claiming ownership in his story, not only of the work of children but also of the work of Black adults, such as Jordan. Even as he credits himself, however, Kohl also documents young people's active shaping of the group. Linda Curry—two years younger than her brother Alvin, Kohl's former student and close collaborator—apparently sought the same support for writing that her brother enjoyed. She gathered a group of peers, including her younger sister Pat, to lobby for a workshop opportunity, prompting Kohl to connect these children with Jordan. The Curry children's organizing set the group up for success. Jordan's teaching notes share her initial worry that no one would show up to the workshop's early meetings, but Linda and Pat filled the room. At the second meeting of the workshop, Pat and Linda casually showed completed writings to Jordan. Already generating texts on their own, Linda and Pat still strategized to procure the resources and opportunities of adult-supported writing. Kohl's declaration that he "got [Jordan] her students" by luring Linda can instead be read as the act of Linda, already a motivated writer, "bugging" or lobbying Kohl until he got a Saturday workshop off the ground.

Children continued to influence the workshop's leadership and structure. Victor Cruz stopped coleading the workshop when it moved from Harlem to a room at the Church of the Open Door in Fort Greene, a Brooklyn neighborhood where most of the participants lived, abutting Bedford-Stuyvesant and a few miles from the Ocean Hill–Brownsville area.[13] Linda Curry had been expelled from, and Pat Curry and other young writers were currently attending, Fort Greene's Sands Junior High School, and these students recruited a teacher there, Terri Bush, to join one Saturday morning. Jordan, born in Brooklyn to Jamaican parents, found an effective codirector in Bush, a white woman recently relocated from Mississippi, who would run the workshop solo in its last year, after Jordan left New York. Jordan and Bush found space and funds for the group's meetings; organized trips and experiences, such as a summer camp; supplied paper, snacks, and books; maintained enough order for writing to occur; served as gatekeepers toward the media and other interested adults; offered models for and ideas about writing; and consulted on spelling and grammar when requested by the children. Jordan and Bush both wrote about the group and preserved relevant papers; I know how the group was structured largely because of adult documentation. In line with T&W's requirement that writer-educators submit weekly "teaching diaries," Jordan provided reflections on each Saturday morning workshop, along with selections of children's literary work, during the group's first year. After the Voice of the Children split with T&W, Jordan continued to write about and keep her own records for the group. Recruiting Bush and arguably recruiting Jordan as well, young people secured the adult support that they deemed productive.

Prompting, shaping, and complementing adults' work, the Curry children and their peers demonstrate an age-based dimension of the literary-historical "importance of associational networks," within which, as Mary Kelley posits, literary production functioned as a "sociable enterprise" across differences of race, class, and gender.[14] While it is easy to narrate the Voice of the Children's founding entirely through adult agency and white-controlled institutions, attending to children's powerful influence exposes the complex, densely social conditions of the group's literary production.

Children collaborated with Jordan to shape the workshop's structure and spirit from its earliest days. Asking children to write about their desires for the group in one of the first Saturday sessions, Jordan reported:

> It is pretty damned clear, from reading what they wrote, that these kids would like to board a Saturday subway and get off at a place like home is supposed to be. They want a kind of permanent inter-attachment to develop among us. We would be a family—swimming when it's hot, going to museums and to places other people go, like Columbia University. The main purpose would be happiness—as a reliable relief from the other six days.[15]

Jordan's repeated use of *would* communicates the willing of the children through her paraphrasing voice. The writers collaboratively author a concept of utopic domesticity that is both fanciful and pragmatic. A few months later, Jordan's notes show this domestic ideal in action: "They really enjoy making a kind of home out of our getting together—writing, talking, laughing, listening to records, hot chocolate and cookies. In fact, one boy, Michael Goode, wrote that Saturdays with the group are when he *lives*."[16] Not only writing within Saturday sessions but authoring the sessions themselves, the group conceived of literary production as an organic part of their domestic project. The interpersonal tensions, off days, and other challenges documented by Jordan in her weekly notes perhaps only deepened the group's sense of their meetings as a "kind of home."

The children's concept of *home* resembles bell hooks's theorization of the "radical political dimension" of "homeplace." Countering male-centric definitions of political struggle, hooks argues that Black women have historically provided domestic environments essential to the work of liberation: "Where all black people could strive to be subjects, not objects, where we would be affirmed in our minds and hearts despite poverty, hardship, and deprivation, where we could restore to ourselves the dignity denied us on the outside in the public world." As in the Voice of the Children's vision of "hot chocolate and cookies," homeplace provides the linked necessities of "the warmth and comfort of shelter, the feeding of our bodies, the nurturing of our souls."[17] Likewise, hooks's portrayal of homeplace as intergenerational, introduced through childhood memories of her grandmother's house, aligns with the Voice of the Children's model. The rooting of homeplace in the work of Black women, moreover, calls attention to Jordan's and other Black women's work of creating environments for youth poetics.

The group's child-shaped, warmly domestic atmosphere nurtured prolific writing. A few months into the workshop, Jordan reported that several members were "quite entirely serious in their determination to become authors of lengthy substance. . . . There are now four books [novels] in progress, i.e.[,] over twenty pages long! Each. At this point, as much writing, or more, takes place between Saturdays!" By 1970, the members were printing a weekly magazine while preparing to publish their anthology—producing both a large quantity and wide variety of literary forms.[18]

If the Voice of the Children represents a best-case scenario for youth writing, that best-case scenario was created not only by the remarkable work of Jordan and other adults but also by the children themselves. These young poets' work, moreover, reflects the warm spirit of the group in surprising ways. The Voice of the Children illustrate hooks's philosophy that to teach and learn with "pleasure" and "excitement" is "to transgress."[19] Rather than using an idyllic environment to craft idyllic poetry, young writers drew on the workshop's sustenance to examine the terms of destruction and despair that dominated the era's public image of young people of color. Even as they expressed real suffering, poets also contested readers' habits and assumptions. And even as they unsettled readership, poets ultimately turned their lines to examine their own voices and selves.

LINDA CURRY'S SECOND-PERSON SELF-WITNESS

Linda (hereafter "Curry") (fig. 2), sister to Alvin and Pat, was involved in the Voice of the Children from about age thirteen to sixteen. Reported by Jordan to be a charismatic leader, who could shift the mood of the group with her personal weather, Curry was elected editor in chief of the Voice of the Children's weekly newspaper and may well have proposed the workshop's name. Jordan's papers from late 1960s are full of references to Curry's prolific work as well as events in her life, which inspired the character of Angela in Jordan's 1971 young adult novel, *His Own Where*. Despite this powerful influence, Curry's work was rarely recognized in 1960s–1970s media coverage and has not received attention from scholars since then. In contrast, Curry's fellow Voice of the Children member Vanessa Howard made such an impression that she published her own individual poetry collection with Holt, Rinehart and Winston in 1972.[20] Curry's work has been overshadowed in part because, whereas Howard's work is legible within dominant conceptions of protest poetry (which I do not mean as disparagement), Curry's verses are short on inspiration as well as overt politics. Curry's sparse publication also clouds appreciation for her.

FIGURE 2. Linda Curry, 1968. © Anna Winand. Featured in *The Voice of the Children*, eds. June Jordan and Terri Bush (New York: Holt, Rinehart and Winston, 1970), 96. —Courtesy of Anna Winand.

Here, I consider two pieces of Curry's unpublished work, as preserved in Jordan's papers, before turning to a poem printed in *The Voice of the Children* anthology. Focusing on Curry's experiments with second-person address helps to clarify her challenging work while also illuminating the larger project of second-person address and poetic relation in the Voice of the Children as a whole. I read Curry within Quashie's conception of the second person as a site for the poetic speaker's own development, discovery, and "self-regard," a process easily overshadowed by preoccupations with oppression, protest, and resistance. Central to Quashie's theory is the implicit point that the "tender becoming of the speaking one" takes shape not only in poems of overt hope—as in Quashie's early example of Jordan's oft-quoted lines, "whoever you are / whoever I may become"—but equally in poetry of devastation, doubt, and despair. Much of Curry's poetry falls in the latter category. Her second-person pessimism invokes readers only to suspend them, casting aside the "burden of audience" to take up the project of her own "self-regard."[21]

Curry expresses this self-fascination through her use of anastrophe, or the inversion of customary word order. Curry's plays with syntactical sequence create a sense of simultaneous directness and distance, suggesting a kind of mindful process of self-investigation even amid direct expressions of pain. An untitled three-stanza poem begins with antique-feeling anastrophe that sidesteps into a despairing vision of the present and future:

> fear have I when it comes
> to another life being
> born into this world
>
> feel the pain of more destruction
> and terror whenever another life
> is added to this thing that
> is called a world [22]

The poet's roundabout phrasing continually turns away, as if directly acknowledging a potential new life would manifest it. "When it comes to": a phrase we use for eventualities we dread. The absoluteness of the speaker's statement—all birth, any birth is bad—plays against ambiguities of subject. The passive tense shrouds birth itself: we don't know who is birthing or being born. This passive confusion is exacerbated by the enjambment of "another life being / born," in which *being* could operate as a gerund, narrating someone *being born*, or as part of a compound noun, describing a *life being*—a more alien form of *human being*. The harsh opening of the second stanza—"feel the pain"—could fall under the first-person subject (*I* feel the pain) or represent a command (*You*: feel the pain). The second-person thus enters halfway, caught at the edges of this chanted spell of negation until the outright hailing of the third stanza:

> I beg of thee
> no more lives to be born
> upon this vegetable
> that is called the Earth.[23]

Direct second-person appeal quickly lapses back into the impersonal passive: "no more lives to be born." Historically the intimate second-person form, *thee* has a paradoxical distancing effect because of its rare use in modern America. Curry's antiquated turns of phrase recall both the moral declarations of Scripture and the alien diction of the era's science fiction, in which otherworldly beings often use antiquated turns of phrase that defamiliarize the failings of twentieth-century American society. Curry's speaker seems to view "this thing that / is called a world," "this vegetable / that is called the Earth" from the distance of outer space. She may be, in the intonations of Sun Ra and his Myth Science Arkestra of the 1960s, creating "interplanetary" art, "travel[ing] the space ways / from planet to planet" in an Afrofuturist leap into other realms of possibility.[24] Curry's despair thus holds a kernel of cosmic thrill, claiming a broad swath of space and time for the first-person speaker even while lamenting her own groundedness.

The poem speaks to the pain fated to the young, pain that the speaker herself seems to have known well. Jordan's papers suggest that this poem makes literal reference to events in the Curry family. But the alien register of the poem prompts caution with such autobiographical reading, particularly given the white American taste for the spectacular pathologizing of Black family life. Indeed, Curry's poem engages this appetite for abjection while subtly twisting its terms into fantasy. Who, after all, could answer the poet's impossible plea? The fear of creating another "life being" suggests the danger associated with bringing another poem into this world, another work of one's own voice vulnerable to misinterpretation and manipulation, what Jodi Melamed terms the "killing sympathies" of liberalism.[25] Yet Curry *is* bringing another poem into this world, one that, even in its nihilism, imaginatively and expressively inhabits what Margo Natalie Crawford identifies in the Black Arts Movement as "a *pregnant* state of anticipation."[26] Returning to Quashie's conception of second-person self-regard, the poet's own act of birthing suggests that she is on some register her own *thee*, one who both begs and refuses, her own most intimate and alien acquaintance. Even as she declares, she asks: Who is the being that I am becoming? Waltzing turns of phrase—"fear have I when it comes," "no more lives to be born"—credit the speaker with the dignity of soliloquy. Her passive voice is not only a failure of the active but also an act of orbiting: inspecting all angles and taking new vantages. This syntactical movement brings *I* and *thee* into relation, turning through the cosmic expanse of the poet's young self.

Curry's self-examination continues even when the first person is entirely absent. Another unpublished, untitled work uses a saturated second person to probe the experience of conditional attention and care. The poem appears here in its entirety:

> When you burn you earn your
>   place in the world
> When you're living your life is
>   like
> a lonely chair in an only room
> When you're dead you're the hero
>   of the world
> And you are forgotten you use to
>   existed   The End.[27]

The refrain, "when you . . ." suggests the vernacular use of *you* as the universal pronoun of aphorisms, as in "you get what you give," or "what you plant now, you'll harvest later." The pairing of the repeated *you* with internal rhymes—burn/earn, life/like, lonely/only—tightens the sense of inevitability in these pronouncements. In Curry's bleak maxims, *you* repeats to the point of parody, straining the assumption of second-person generalities: that the speaker and listener experience things in the same way.

Like Phillip Solomon's "black child, / step in the back," Curry's single stanza warns a second-person addressee of the pitfalls of visibility politics. Curry equates the US ideal of meritocracy—the idea of "earn[ing] your place in the world"—with the terms of public attention and reputation in the 1960s. The phrase "[w]hen you burn you earn" also hints at "burn baby burn," a slogan associated with the 1965 Watts uprising. In the idea of achievement through suffering, the line evokes late 1960s criticisms of the civil rights tactics of nonviolent resistance. Curry's imagery may also call up the literal burning of Vietnam under US military fire, as well as the figure of Thich Quang Duc, a Buddhist monk who died in Saigon by self-immolation on June 11, 1963, to protest the persecution of Buddhists in South Vietnam. What resonates here is not only these events themselves but their spectacular coverage on television, context that deepens Curry's concern with the terms of American publicity. Bringing this transnational context to the locality of Brooklyn childhood, the concept of *earning by burning* names the national appetite for stories of children's oppression. Curry sparks the question of whether the poem itself is a flame, attracting attention in proportion to the heat of its trauma. In this light, the second person may invite readers to examine their own motives for consuming the work of Curry and her peers.

But *you* repeats in excess of this readerly reckoning. Reveling in the act of invocation, the poet abstracts the second person beyond any specific audience. The poem's arc of pronouns—*you-you-your-you're-your-you're-you're-you-you*—suggests a path of descent and return. The route follows the temporal and conditional openings of "When . . ." With every *when*, *you* takes on a new imagery and setting. The result is a quick sequence of metaphors and circumstances, which simultaneously increase the poem's claustrophobia and hint at mobility. There is a sense of investigation here, of iterative testing, through which the speaker implicitly emerges as an observer who both identifies with and holds at a distance the terrible fate of *you*. Perhaps the second person is the poet's projection of a public self, and the very act of defining this self's fate opens space for imagining first-person possibility.

This sense of space increases even in the harsh foreclosure of the poem's concluding couplet:

> And you are forgotten you use to
> existed The End.

Curry uses verb conjugations to shape a distinct flow of narrative time. Her placement of the suffix *-ed*, "you use to existed," contrasts with the White Mainstream English convention "you used to exist." Curry's wording employs the Black Language practice of "voiceless final consonant clusters," as in *use* over *used*, and places the emphasis of the past tense on *existed*, in line with the preceding past participle, *forgotten*.[28] Echoing the internal rhymes of the previous lines, this doubling of past participles intensifies the feeling of loss. The speaker suggests something like "your existence is forgotten" and, simultaneously, "you've forgotten your own existence"; the difficulty of explication here reflects the impossibility of discussing one's own absence. Curry's line "you are forgotten you use to / existed" serves as the concluding example of the specific power of Black English in a 1972 essay by Jordan. "There is no adequate, standard English translation possible for [Curry's] expression of her spirit," Jordan writes. Curry's lines "are intrinsically Black language cries of extreme pain so telling that even the possibilities of meaning and existence have been formulated in a past tense that is emphatic, severe." Curry's second-person temporal sculpting allows Jordan to demonstrate how Black English holds "elements of the spirit that have provided for our survival."[29]

Jordan's commentary suggests how Curry's expressions of despair and disappearance also assert her poetic presence. The enjambment of "to/existed" gives *existed* its own existence, suggesting isolation but possibly also a life that mattered. Pauses between words could denote the silence of the forgotten dead or invite a breath of open possibility. The speaker leaves a space, or loophole, between the elegiac past of "existed" and the theatrical "The End." This last phrase only reminds us that the overt story has been over from the first line of the poem, "When you burn . . ." The poem performs the poet's ability to speak past the terms of social life, to preserve the present-tense flow of experience and of creation.

Curry's unpublished investigations of first- and second-person dynamics set the stage for a work printed in *The Voice of the Children* anthology. The poem "for Nina Simone wherever you are" applies the lessons of Curry's previous works in a strikingly different atmosphere, moving from overt trauma to joy. Curry joins the Black Arts practice of crafting odes to musicians, such as K. William Kgositsile's own poem for Simone, "Ivory Masks in Orbit," published in the groundbreaking Black Arts anthology *Black Fire*.[30] Such works allowed poets to investigate the sometimes-fraught relationship between music and writing and to explore the musical possibilities of written verse. In Curry's own work, a shifting second person turns her ode to Simone into a celebration of the poet's own voice, merging the acts of hearing and of creating the sound of Black women's freedom.

for Nina Simone   wherever you are

The great
                singer
                                Nina Simone
        fills your heart with soul
        she makes your brain rock and roll
        makes your mind forget
                        the question that is unanswered

Go ahead Nina bring
                out all of your black soul
        Just sing it
                hit it to the
                white man eyes
        Make him realize
        that a black woman voice
                            will never
                                    die[31]

From the first words, this poem performs a looseness that is far from the claustrophobia of "fear have I" and "When you burn." The tight-mouthed consonant clusters of the latter work—*burn, earn, only, lonely*—give way to a rush of breath with the open calls of *fill, heart, soul, Go ahead*. Curry reproduces the way a single bar of a song can loosen a body. Even the spacing of the poem on the page, the easy swing to the right of "great / singer / Nina Simone," suggests a dancer's joy in taking up space. This joyful experience of the first stanza belongs to the second person. The use of *you* captures the experience of being sung *to*: listening, receiving, being under Simone's spell. It is a spell that allows for spaciousness, moving across the lines' sibilant *s* sounds, moving with Simone "wherever you are."

The second stanza reverses this dynamic with the imperative "Go ahead Nina." Simone now occupies the second person, receiving the urgings of the poetic speaker. By shifting Simone into the receiving position of *you*, the poet asserts her own identity as an artist, who is not only inspired by but may also give inspiration to Simone. Though Simone ostensibly sings to "hit it to the / white man eyes / Make him realize," the sensory mismatch of singing toward eyes, rather than ears, suggests the white man is beside the point. Chances are slim that he will hear through his eyes and truly "realize" anything. The relevant character here is the poet herself, who *realizes* her own version of "a black woman voice." Through the shifting second person, Curry expresses a musical give and take, capturing the way in which witnessing another artist can put one in touch with the power of their own voice.

Though the above reading sets audience aside in favor of the poet's self-listening, the invocation of Simone presents an opportunity to reconsider readership. Curry honors an artist known for, as Daphne Brooks explains, a "uniquely tense push and pull with her audiences." In live concert records, everyday fans could hear Simone deploy such tactics as addressing Black audience members specifically, sardonically calling attention to listeners' ill-timed laughter, and directing them when to applaud. Through "performative distanciation," Brooks argues, Simone "challeng[ed] her audiences to consider and perhaps more importantly to listen for the meaning of liberation in black female performance."[32] Simone crafted her own musicality of liberation not *despite* but *through* sometimes-tense encounters with listeners and the likely constant experience of being misheard and misunderstood. By folding these encounters into the content of her music, the singer thus offers a model for young writers like Curry, who negotiated interracial groups of adult support-ers and fans in spaces analogous to Simone's Carnegie Hall.

Curry's own "push and pull" emerges through her use of second-person address. Whereas the first stanza seems to invite all readers into an implied collective *you*, the second stanza evicts readers from that *you* in favor of Simone. Curry goes on to name the poles of the third-person "white man" and implied first-person "black woman," between which readers presumably position themselves. Regardless of this placement, the withdrawal of second-person identification creates an unstable reading experience, prompting audiences to question their own position.

This unsettling is compounded by a problem in the first stanza. Simone's voice, the poet promises, "makes your mind forget / the question that is unanswered." The question is not only unanswered but also unasked, leav-ing an open question about the question. What kind of question would be forgotten through the voice of Simone, who continually posed questions, raised challenges, and insisted on remembrance? And how can we forget a question that remains hanging in the air? Perhaps Curry alludes to a ques-tion that she chooses not to dignify with response, in line with W. E. B. Du Bois's indelible passage: "Between me and the other world there is ever an unasked question. . . . To the real question, How does it feel to be a problem? I answer seldom a word."[33] Like Du Bois, Curry crafts her own voice around the shadow of the undisclosed. The parallel conclusions of the two stanzas link "the question that is unanswered" with "a black woman voice," suggesting that the voice may not only endure despite the question but even draw power from that which remains unsettled and unresolved.

Through plays with second-person address, Curry witnesses herself in the act of poetic expression. In the very process of critiquing attention and unsettling readership, this poet investigates her own mobility and authority.

MICHAEL GOODE'S AND CHRISTOPHER MEYER'S INTERROGATIONS OF POETIC AUTHORITY

Linda Curry's second-person verses contribute to a larger interrogation of poetic address among the Voice of the Children writers. *I/you* dynamics structure what is perhaps the group's most circulated poem, which helped draw publicity and support for the Voice of the Children in its first year. On April 4, 1968, members of the Voice of the Children attended an evening poetry reading by June Jordan and Clarence Major at the East Village artistic hub St. Mark's Church. After hearing the news of the shooting of Martin Luther King, Jr., Jordan and Major had decided to continue with the reading in King's honor. Several of the children, meanwhile, had heard the news on TV at Terri Bush's home, immediately began writing poetry, and continued that writing when they arrived at Jordan and Major's reading. Twelve-year-old Michael Goode's poem "April 4 1968" likely emerged from this moment of real-time intergenerational poetic exchange.[34] Goode's elegy appeared in the *Village Voice* the next week and subsequently in multiple anthologies, and it is likely that Goode shared the poem in one or more of the Voice of the Children's radio and TV appearances.[35]

The heart of Goode's verse is its mingling of authority and vulnerability. Goode uses first- and second-person voice, as well as pointedly colloquial interjections, to examine what happens to language itself during great loss and upheaval.

> war war
> why do god's children fight among each other
> like animals
> a great man once lived
> a Negro man
> his name was the Rev. Martin Luther King.
>
> but do you know what happened?
> he was assasinated by a white man.[36]

This first call to *you*, "but do you know what happened?," sets a demanding tone of second-person address. The speaker seems to be processing the events by insistently confronting *you* with them.

> yes
> that's courage
> when you fight back of course you're brave
> but do you think you yourself can stand up
> and let someone beat you
>
> [. . . .]
>
> shot him down
> that's right
> one of God's children[37]

You is the vessel of the speaker's reckoning. While *you* may represent Goode's inner dialogue, the colloquial second person also suggests the effort to come into conversation with other people in a moment of dramatic social and political reorganization. In questioning and challenging the second person, the speaker acquires an air of authority: "yes / that's courage," "that's right." Colloquial interjections call attention to the act of speaking truth, as the poet explores his own capacity to find words in the wake of something terrible. The poet's declarations concern the future as well as the past: "well you can count on a long hot summer." A "hot summer" of unrest is not much of a prospect to "count on," but on April 4, 1968, complete certainty and utter uncertainty coexist.

This dissonance shapes the arrival of the overt first person late in the poem:

> I will long remember this dark day.
> it's funny it's so you can't even
> walk out in the street anymore
> some maniac might shoot you
> in cold blood.
>
> what kind of a world is this?
>
> I don't know.[38]

While the initial first-person declaration, "I will long remember," seems definitive, the subject of memory seems to make the speaker falter. An uncharacteristic understatement introduces a stumbling rhythm: "it's funny it's so you can't even . . ." The speaker can't make it even, can't even it out.

Here, as in the earlier stanza on courage, the second person is explicitly bared to threat. The poet insists on the immediate and personal consequences of King's death. In these last lines of the poem, second-person exposure drops the poet into the first-person *I*. Three standalone lines suggest pauses of solitary contemplation; the length of stanzas has diminished over the course of the poem. We are down to the heart of things, where the poet gathers the authority to declare his own unknowing.

Goode's mingling of first and second person, challenge and vulnerability, give "April 4 1968" a tonal balance of warmth and distance that proved appealing for broad circulation. Goode's poem was not alone. King's death and the consequent Holy Week Uprising—the nationwide outbreak of protests and police responses to them that ended in forty-three deaths, thousands of injuries, and twenty-seven thousand arrests, drove adult readers to young people's writings.[39] At least two full anthologies from 1968 focused on children's responses to the assassination and its aftermath, while other anthologies featured individual writings on the topic.[40] These texts offered a fresh perspective on events to readers of wide-ranging political stances, because of the broad reputation of children's writings for unmatched, unfiltered honesty. Goode's poem, with its frank, authoritatively uncertain tone, both answered and unsettled the popular desire for some definitive speaking of truth. Adults variously deferred to, reshaped, and preserved Goode's poem as they circulated it. Terri Bush, who was likely a classroom teacher of Goode, recalled in a 1970 interview: "People get uptight whenever children are taken seriously. They think we are involved in some kind of disruptive plot. At Sands Junior High, the principal and school officials [were] extremely upset over the [reading] in an assembly of one of our member's poems describing the assassination of Dr. King," she said. "They were terrified that it would cause a riot which would be blamed entirely on the 12-year-old girl [i.e., Michael Goode]. But it was really a beautiful poem."[41]

Interviewed on the publication of *The Voice of the Children* anthology, Bush recalls the reception of Goode's poem in order to prime potential readers of the book. Though Bush does not name Goode, the journalist who interviewed her does name "April 4 1968"; the attribution of the poem to a "girl" could reflect Michael's actual gender or an error. Bush's image of school administrators' fear and disapproval advertises the antiestablishment thrill of the anthology. In contrast, Bush presents Goode's work as "beautiful" and peaceful.

Goode's poem found both powerful publicity and potentially undermining framings in early printings. For instance, T&W director Zelda Wirtshafter used "April 4 1968" to address King's death in the following week's *Teachers & Writers Collaborative Newsletter*, a robust magazine still active today. In her preface to the T&W magazine issue, Wirtshafter presents Goode's poem as "a concrete affirmation of our hope and ultimate goal for the teaching of English, i.e.[,] that children should find in the English classroom a place where they can confront their immediate concerns openly and honestly and begin to explore these concerns both through their own creative expression and through contact with the larger literary culture."[42] While Wirtshafter laudably shares her platform with Goode, she subsumes the substance of his verse under the category of personal, "immediate concerns," which can at most "begin" to achieve aesthetic form. Wirtshafter thus follows a common tendency of uncritical reception to youth writing, which I detail in chapter 4. Framing Goode as a beneficiary of English pedagogy, Wirtshafter elides her own position as a white adult beneficiary of Goode's work: she depends on the poet to provide the right words to meet tragedy and crisis.

The popularity of "April 4 1968" provided the Voice of the Children with an early lesson in the rewards and risks of public writing. Goode's reception surfaced the pitfalls of visibility that Jordan, Curry, and Solomon would challenge, as white adults in particular framed and interpreted Goode's work in sometimes discrediting ways. But Goode's verse was well equipped to manage such circumstances. The poem itself reframes interracial and intergenerational attention by modeling an interrogation into the nature of authority and truth-telling, plying the space between "Well you can count on . . ." and "I don't know." By enacting its own dialogue about right response, Goode's poem transcends the terms of its circulation and reception.

The Voice of the Children, like other youth writing fora, confronted questions about the role of error in children's texts. The stakes of this issue emerge in another reprinting of "April 4 1968" by a white adult. Like Wirtshafter, critic Nat Hentoff turned to Goode's words in the week after King's death, within Hentoff's media-watchdog column, "Review of the Press," in the prominent alternative newspaper the *Village Voice*. Hentoff's April 11 column, which responds to King's death by condemning the negligent coverage of racism and anti-racism by the Associated Press, features Goode's full poem as well as a segment of prose that Goode apparently wrote in school on April 5: "There was once a day when I used to say that Martin Luther King was nothing, but a day came when, when, everybody had to eat there words because he was dead. Shot with a hot rot grin." Bush likely passed these lines and "April 4 1968" to Hentoff, who was involved in local school reform and would later join T&W. Within Hentoff's column, Goode's poetry and prose stand as an implicit corrective to media dishonesty, as if to say: this is what truth telling sounds like. Hentoff borrows Goode's words to title that week's column, "Shot with a Hot Rot Grin."[43] Suggesting the crack of gunfire with -ot rhymes, Goode's phrase recalls the sinister smile of Batman's Joker and the speed of a *hot rod* car—both popular images in late 1960s television—as well as the *rot* of moral decay. Goode thus provides a vivid term for the smug impunity of white American power of which Hentoff accuses the press and the state.

Though thematically resonant with his poem, Goode's prose sets a different tone because of its proximity to childish error. Hentoff's preservation of Goode's use of *there* for *their*, as in "eat there words," may be construed as either honoring Goode's literacy or flagging its fallibility, reinforcing the common tendency to value youth writing as unvarnished emotion, rather than craft. Indeed, child authors' orthography was a subject of heated debate among adult supporters of 1960s–1970s youth writing. Within T&W, Phillip Lopate recalls, the question of whether and how to correct children's spelling and grammar became known as "The Great Spelling Question." Correction, some argued, could repress children's expressive freedom and destructively impose white, middle-class norms. A lack of correction, however, could become condescending and voyeuristic, indulging an appetite for the gritty authenticity of impoverished youth.[44] Prominent child author Kali Grosvenor, for instance, resented the publication of her misspellings, as she later told scholar Katharine Capshaw.[45] Priding themselves on their antiestablishment radicality, adult collaborators feared their own potentially heavy-handed power. The spelling debate raged on in T&W for years, "and with such anxiety that it was clearly the tip of some iceberg or other."[46] The bulk of this iceberg was the racial politics of language.

Questions of children's orthography intersected with the Black Arts Movement's commitment to nationalist language forms unbound to White Mainstream English's aesthetic and grammatical norms. The linguistic nature of Black Power is clear in Stokely Carmichael's 1966 vow: "For once, black people are going to use the words they want to use—not just the words whites want to hear."[47] The growing use of Black English in published literature, as well as in classrooms, opened new possibilities for children's writing but also fears of inauthentic co-optation and caricature. Additional opportunities emerged through Latinx literary engagements with bilingualism and vernaculars. The white identities of many adult teachers and supporters of youth writing likely ensnared them in such questions of language. In my own experience as a white scholar, I can fail to discern Black Language poetics, and my whiteness can inappropriately center problems of interraciality in my literary interpretations.

In the Voice of the Children, writers requested adult technical consultations as desired. Children asked grammatical questions as they arose and could take or leave the answers, and the writers as a group eventually decided to institute the correction of spelling errors for the sake of clarity. Jordan and Bush repeatedly argued that their children's-choice policy made the Great Spelling Question a nonissue.[48] Jordan's explanation of the policy in the anthology afterword subtly critiques the adult preoccupation: "Spelling is one problem [the workshop writers] want to solve; they want to avoid adult errors of understanding; they want people to receive the message, and no mistake about it."[49] Jordan categorizes misunderstandings as characteristically *adult* and places the burden of error on the interpreter, rather than the writer. She defends the space for the young writers' authorial agency while also implying that young writers have something to teach adults about communication.

While the experience of Goode's publicity, including the preservation of his spelling in the *Village Voice*, may have shaped the Voice of the Children's subsequent decisions, Goode and his peers also examined literary accuracy through verse. Goode's prose and a poem by his fellow Voice of the Children poet Christopher Meyer shift the debate about children's orthography by poetically examining the very concept of error.

The theme of error and correction drives Goode's passage: "There was once a day when I used to say that Martin Luther King was nothing, but a day came when, when, everybody had to eat there words because he was dead. Shot with a hot rot grin." In Goode's narration, the experience of changing one's perspective and repenting an old belief is tied to the assassination, as if one's personal dismissal of King's ideas contributed to his death. The repulsive terms of the killing, reflected in the image of grinning rot, cast a sickening light on the speaker's mistake. The feeling here is not only grief but visceral wrongness. The eating of one's words—an idiom often used lightly—here takes on its full stomach-turning strangeness. The spelling of "there words" adds to the wrong feeling—illustrating how rhetorical context shapes the consequences of orthography.

Like his poetry, which loops back to words and phrases in a rhythm modeling natural thought, Goode's prose is structured by iteration: "There was once a day . . . but a day came." Mirroring this pairing of days, the doubling of "when, when" emphasizes how the speaker must pause and reconsider his own thought in a watershed moment. Goode's motif of iteration cultivates an understanding of literary authority as dynamic and processual. This emphasis on the act of reexamination aligns with the contemplative shifts of "April 4 1968," as Goode explores the concept of truth telling through a delicate weave of authority and vulnerability, *you* and *I*.

Extending Goode's interest in error, a poem by ten-year-old Christopher Meyer, June Jordan's son, pushes the limits of coherence in a scathing survey of what his city's adults have gotten wrong.

> Wonderful New York
>
> The hypnotizing neon light
> the street banks like garbage dumps
> and the drunk vacuum cleaner
> who suck up whiskey like air
> converts my mind into a
> cemetery of the noisy
>
> As New York provides a building for the U.N.
> so shall it provide its cemetery
> Invisible dangers are always around the corner,
> as hell is around the corner for me.[50]

Chaotically overlapping figures of speech create a darkly fantastic mood evocative of film noir and dystopic representations of American city life. After a barely figural simile—street banks are literally places where garbage gets dumped—comes the combined metaphor-simile of a drunk person who *is* a vacuum cleaner, sucking up whiskey *like* air. This figural jumble mimics the environment that "converts my mind into a / cemetery of the noisy." The singular-plural reversal of the verb *converts*, rather than *convert*, with *suck up*, rather than *sucks up*, reflects the "hypnotizing" tangle of the preceding images, which seem to cause mental distortion. Perhaps both the street banks and the drunk are sucking up whisky; perhaps it is the "neon light" that "converts my mind," as if lines 2 through 4 never happened. Figural and grammatical ambiguity replicate the poet's mental experience of "a cemetery of the noisy." Does the speaker experience a noisy cemetery, full of both the racket and the desolate loneliness of the city? Or is the poet's mind a place where noise goes to die? The confusion increases with the second stanza's chiasmus of analogies: "as . . . so . . . as." The poet leverages repeated words and the imprecision of *as*—conjunction, preposition, or adverb?—to pull toward a conclusion that seems both illogical and undeniable: "as hell is around the corner for me."

The poet's position at the edge of coherence reveals the city itself as a landscape of error. The "cemetery of the noisy," which could be either a noisy place of death or a place where noise has died, transmutes in the second stanza into the city itself. Manhattan's bleakly affluent landscape of skyscrapers appears as a skyline of gravestones—presaging the cemetery imagery of Jordan's 1971 young adult novel, *His Own Where*. Prominent on that skyline, particularly as viewed from the Voice of the Children's home base of Brooklyn, are the headquarters of the United Nations. Completed in 1952, a few years before Meyer's birth, this massive complex took on ironic symbolic weight during the Vietnam War. Meyer maps a landscape literally shaped by the corruption and moral errors of adults in power. He turns the tables on the Great Spelling Question by highlighting the errors of adults, not children. It is adult wrongdoing that turns the city into a dangerous and desolate place for the young speaker, a place in which he cannot afford a misstep.

JUNE JORDAN'S SHAPING OF ADULT AGENCY

Young writers' defense against the destructive force of adult error found a crucial collaborator in June Jordan. Throughout her years with the Voice of the Children, Jordan worked to defend and champion the physical and conceptual space of children's poetics. In the process, she created a critical framework for understanding the children's work—a framework in conversation with young writers' own presentations of themselves. The deep resonances between Jordan's writings on the group and the workshop members' poetry indicate a collaborative project of nurturing and theorizing children's poetics.

Jordan and Bush found that maintaining the environment of the workshop required active management of the potentially heavy hand of adult support. The directors produced a steady stream of correspondence to actively recruit new fans, arrange for readings and other publicity, seek out resources for the children, and protest poor treatment of them. For instance, a letter from Bush to the president of Volkswagen asks the company to donate a bus to the group; Jordan, meanwhile, sent a complaint to the president of Chock full o'Nuts protesting discrimination faced by the children at one of the company's shops. The directors, then, worked both to pull adults into the group's orbit and to push against them.[51]

Many, though not all, of the adult supporters of the workshop were middle-class and white. Adult fans provided the workshop with organizational resources, publicity, and money, especially given the group's constant funding struggles, which would contribute to its 1971 demise.[52] In turn, progressive New York adults such as photographer Anna Winand—who took the photographs of writers used in *The Voice of the Children* anthology, including the portrait of Linda Curry featured here—and writer-editor Millen Brand found rewards in intimacy with the group.[53] As Ellen Jaffe recalls, after hosting the Voice of the Children writers on her local radio show, "I was hooked. Drawn in by their heartfelt poems, by June's dynamic presence and Terri's quiet assurance, I found myself working with the group every Saturday."[54] Balancing children's literary freedom with adult supporters' engagement would require teaching the latter how to behave.

To shape adults' agency within the workshop, Jordan developed guidelines for "Visitors and Adult Friends of the Children." In a typewritten document, Jordan reminds fans that "[t]his is a children's workshop, striving to serve the growing interests and abilities of the children, exclusively." The necessity of reiterating this point suggests the visitors' tendency to forget it. Five guidelines describe proper conduct within "a children's workshop." Adults should participate in the workshop just as young members do, by "conversing with children, reading books, or by writing." The document discourages "adult-to-adult conversation," particularly comments about the children and their work in their presence. Discussion of the directors' pedagogical techniques "should be reserved for some separate, adult-to-adult occasion." When children share their work, visitors should neither correct nor "excessive[ly] praise" it. The final rule admonishes, "Please do not attempt to 'look over the shoulder' of children while they are writing; creative expression of oneself requires a modicum of privacy."[55] As a delegate to her fellow adults, Jordan negotiates between the normative adult-to-adult world and the adult-to-child encounters that presumably attracted visitors to the workshop. Even as the guidelines set the vectors of the audible adult voice and visible adult gaze, they also refer to external exchanges, with topics "reserved for some separate, adult-to adult occasion." The goal of the guidelines, then, is not to abolish the Goffmanian "backstage" of adult interchange but to increase its discretion to prevent damaging the children's writing process. Visitors must be made aware of their potential effect, learning to watch themselves watch and catching themselves acting on common impulses, such as peering over children's shoulders. Teaching adults conscious self-restraint, the guidelines aim to maintain a balance of child and adult agencies that can support young writers.

Jordan makes clear the stakes of this balance in a February 1968 letter to Wirtshafter, the T&W director who would publish Goode's poem in the group's magazine two months later. Jordan's letter delivers a sharp lesson on the potentially destructive effects of aesthetic judgments on children's writing. Apparently responding to Wirtshafter's suggestion that Robert Louis Stevenson was an inappropriate model for one workshop poet, Jordan writes:

> One should take care to discover racist ideas that are perhaps less obvious than others. For example, one might ask: Will I accept that a black child can write "creatively" and "honestly" and yet *not* write about incest, filth, violence and degradations of every sort? Back of the assumption, and there is an assumption, that an honest and creative piece of writing by a black child will be ungrammatical, mis-spelled, and lurid titillation for his white teacher, is another idea. That black people are only the products of racist, white America and that, therefore, we can be and we can express only what racist white America has forced us to experience, namely: mutilation, despisal, ignorance and horror. . . . There really are black children who dream, and who love, and who undertake to master such white things as poetry. There really are black children who are *children* as well as victims. And one had better be pretty damned careful about what one will "accept" from these children as their own—their own honest expression of their dreams, their love, and their always human reality that not even America can conquer.[56]

Jordan roots stylistic questions about children's poetry in fundamental matters of humanity. She links the perception of poetic diction to 1960s culture-of-poverty arguments, which pathologized Black people in the guise of social science. Her image of a white teacher awaiting "lurid titillation" from a Black child writer identifies the stereotypical image of youth writing, one that Jordan's own presence contests. Her sarcastic use of quotation marks around "creatively," "honestly" and "accept" announces that as Wirtshafter evaluated a child's poetry, so will Jordan scrutinize the words of Wirtshafter and other white adult readers. As in her workshop guidelines, Jordan turns the spotlight back onto privileged adults' practices of reading.

Even while prompting adult visitors' self-scrutiny, Jordan also sheds light on her own role in the work of youth writing. We might view Jordan as young writers' protector. Using her words to defend the space of young writers' words, perhaps Jordan sought to spare children the labor and distraction of their own defense. But as the writings of Solomon, Curry, Goode, and Meyer make clear, young writers were ready to confront, rather than escape, the micro- and macroaggressions of white adult readers. These poets knew how to use their collective home of "hot chocolate and cookies" to compose portraits of destruction and despair. Young writers deftly turned threats—including the soft vice of adult fans' misreadings—into the settings for poetic examinations of self. Jordan's works of protest and protection contributed to the Voice of the Children's collective investigation of the value, possibilities, and optimal support of children's poetics.

The Voice of the Children's name, selected by the young writers themselves, may register as dissonant with twenty-first-century critiques of *voice*. Post–World War II US culture, Jodi Melamed argues, has subsumed anti-racisms into "permissible narratives of difference" through processes of political and social recognition: "Forms of humanity *win their rights, enter into representation,* or *achieve a voice* at the same moment that the normative model captures and incorporates them" into the liberal-capitalist US order.[57] In other words, the articulation and reception of *voice* can promote a reductionist approach to literary work and elide actual challenges to power.

Melamed's critique resonates with the suspicion of public attention that pervades works by Solomon, Curry, and their peers. While *The Voice of the Children* accesses the power of voice as a cultural concept, the group's name also self-consciously revises that dynamic. Whereas the liberal concept of voice is closely tied to the first person, the group's young writers chose to name themselves in the third person. Their title strikes a contrast to the first-person titles of many contemporaneous youth writing anthologies: *The Me Nobody Knows; I Am Somebody!; Somebody Real; Here I Am!*[58] Some of these titles were chosen by children, some were taken from children's writings, and others were dreamed up by adult editors. According to these titles, broadcasting young people's first-person voices is by nature political, inherently an act of resistance. The titles may encourage a biographical interpretation of all the anthologized texts, even those that are far from life writing. Children's voices are presented as transparent, self-asserting, and self-locating: *Here I Am!* The Voice of the Children reappropriates this discourse by making a bold claim to the category of childhood from the self-conscious distance of the third person. The name indicates children's interest in their own poetic subjectivities. Solomon, Curry, Goode, Meyer, and their peers were carefully investigating the risks and possibilities of writing under public attention. These poets aimed not only to "achieve a voice" for political recognition but also to know their own collective and varied voice, for their own sake.

The Voice of the Children provides a remarkable model for youth writing—not because of the absence of microaggressions or co-optations but because of the collective ways in which children and adults like Jordan challenged those threats and leveraged them toward children's own expressive force. Interpreting the group's poetics in light of its challenges sets a foundation for appreciating texts from more overtly problematic and compromised sites of youth writing, which I explore in the next two chapters.

CHAPTER 2

Telling Time
Anti-Racist Temporalities in the Classroom

On May 4th 1968 a girl decided to write about her opinions of ways to fight. I don't mean fist fight but I mean fight with your mind. . . . You must fight with your brain and you have got to know how to do it. You can use your brain differently.

Carmen begins her essay "You've Got to Fight the Right Way," which gives this chapter its epigraph, by commemorating her own act of composition.[1] She dates her essay exactly one month after the April 4 assassination of Martin Luther King, Jr. Her meditation on the power of fighting without fists references King's commitment to nonviolence, even at a time of increasing debates about the right "ways to fight" for anti-racist change. As a strategy document for struggle, Carmen's essay shows affinity with texts such as the 1969 "13 Point Program and Platform" of the Young Lords, a movement of Puerto Rican revolutionaries in mainland US cities.[2] Carmen's discussion of resistance tactics and her self-conscious narration of authorship connect through the theme of time. Shifting quickly between past and present tenses, Carmen positions temporal markers at the center of her discussion of survival tactics. Her self-conscious timestamp, "On May 4th 1968," presents the production of the essay itself as a historical event in the tradition of "fight[ing] with your mind." She links her timestamp, moreover, to the timebound nature of child authorship: one is not "a girl" forever, but Carmen was "a girl" precisely on May 4, 1986, when she "decided to write." Carmen demonstrates an age-specific form of anti-racist temporality.

If Western culture shapes stories around beginning, middle, and end, to set those temporal markers is to control a story's meaning. Carmen fights with her mind partly by asserting the starting point of her own text. As a public school student writer, she also strategically chose to share her essay with her sixth-grade writing teacher, Caroline Mirthes. Mirthes then included the work in her popular 1971 collection of writings from her students at the Lower East Side's PS 15, *Can't You Hear Me Talking to You?* The volume also featured writing by Carmen's friend Elisa, which opens the introduction of this book. In the hands of their teacher-turned-editor, Carmen's and Elisa's writing would operate along an adult-directed timeline of circulation and interpretation. Anthologies from single classrooms, as opposed to collections from multiple schools or from extracurricular programs, present child authorship within the bounded space and nine-month time of the public school class. The adult teacher-editor's power manifests sequentially: in her ability to have the last word, to explain in retrospect, and to publish and copyright a book long after the writers have left her classroom. In this light, Carmen's commemorative opening, "On May 4th 1968," seems to anticipate and counterbalance a textual life outside of the young writer's control.

The stakes of this timing become visible in a 1971 *New York Times* feature on the publication of *Can't You Hear Me Talking to You?* Following excerpts of children's writings from the book, the article concludes with "An Epilogue" in which Mirthes gives a "résumé of the present situation of some of the writers." The report on Carmen, quoted here in its entirety, is typical: "CARMEN has bleached her long black hair blond and wears a black slit skirt and a low-cut top. She lives with her mother, who has a 19-year-old boyfriend. They live in a one-room flat where the furnishings consist of a bed and a couch and the sink is in the living room."[3] Mirthes makes no mention of Carmen's writing or interior world. The focus is on Carmen's body, the corruption of which mirrors the deviant sexuality of her mother and improper state of their apartment. Carmen's "black slit skirt" and "low-cut top" appear directly expressive of her current existence. The costume marks her fall from childhood innocence—and thus from the realm of child authorship. In line with explicit claims in the "résumé" that other former students have abandoned artistic pursuits, from dropping the trumpet to discarding dreams of a writing career, Mirthes implies that Carmen, too, has lost her creative ability. Declaring Carmen's window of literary production closed, the article offers up her body as a substitute text for readers' consumption. The *Times* "epilogue" extends the work already begun in the concluding pages of *Can't You Hear Me Talking to You?*, in which Mirthes reports the dropouts, pregnancies, and drug overdoses that have struck students since leaving her class, expressing their urgent need for help but also narratively reassuring readers that they have not missed anything beyond the anthology's last page.[4]

Mirthes exemplifies a central tendency of adult narratives about youth writing: to age children of color out of authorship. She retrospectively constructs her own classroom as the exceptional space of childhood and, by extension, child literary production, shielded by age from what she terms the "disaster area" of the Lower East Side.[5] Young people, in this account, are children only as long as they are her students, and writers only as long as they are children. By luridly portraying the changes of time and growth, the *Times* epilogue reinforces young writers' disqualification from childhood, from authorship, and thus from a claim to their own published texts.

In a second temporal move, the *Times* not only fails to solicit young writers' own input but also assumes the impossibility of their ever seeing the article. The tone of the résumé excludes its own subjects' readership as confidently as a social worker's case file: "IRENE has regressed socially. She appears afraid of growing up because she does not know how to deal with drugs and sex."[6] By denying Irene, Carmen, and their peers and families as potential readers, the article constructs the conversation about young people of color as a one-way stream, in which provocative material moves from children's lives and pens up into the teacher's possession, then on to editors, publishers, and a privileged adult public. The *Times*' assumption of a one-way stream follows the anthology itself, which Mirthes dedicates to the children but peppers with statements about them and their families that seem confident of a complete lack of community reception.

Can't You Hear Me Talking to You? and its newspaper epilogue exert narrative control over children's past and future, shaping claims both to explain and to predict their lives. This adult discourse around child authors has a structural affinity with a form of narrative widespread in the circa-1970 era: the pathologization of poverty, which renders oppression as the inevitable result of oppressed people's own dysfunction, fully explainable by simple causality. The application of pathology discourse to children of color is exemplified in the circa-1970 policing term "predelinquent," which preemptively targeted young people based solely on their perceived proclivity for future crimes.[7] Drawing on Michael King's theorization of "the protocols of telling" in this era, I argue that Carmen and her fellow classroom writers actively contest what I call *time-telling*: a form of domination that uses temporal logic to tell a story about another's identity and future.[8]

The young writers examined in this chapter demand a distinct approach to the temporal mapping of race-, class-, gender-, and age-based structures of power. Rachel Conrad's study of temporality in child authorship challenges the developmental framework that conceives of children's artistry as valuable not in its own right but instead as evidence of the potential for real, adult artistry in the future. This framework rests on "mental judgments about children as 'less' (capable, logical, thoughtful) than adults."[9] This developmental teleology, however, has not been universally applied. In Carmen's time and place, pervasive racist thought associated Black and Latinx people's coming of age with devolution and threat, so that it was adults, rather than children, who were assumed to be *less*. The narrative of writers' aging out of authorship reveals how childhood can operate as a culturally exceptional space, even as youth also compounds race and class marginalization.

Equating maturation with loss, the concept of aging out of authorship adapts the deep-seated cultural ideal of Romantic childhood. Iconicized in William Wordsworth's 1807 "Ode: Intimations of Immortality," canonical Romantic thought defines childhood through its inaccessibility to the adult poet, who mourns a "lost sense of potential," as Linda Austin explains.[10] Whereas Robin Bernstein has traced non-white children's widespread and destructive exclusion from the Romantic ideal of childhood innocence, white adults' treatment of 1960s–1970s young authors like Carmen reveals a contrasting process.[11] The logic of aging out of authorship emphatically applies Romantic childhood—and thus, a mourning for its inevitable loss—to Black and Puerto Rican young people. This process reveals how selective inclusion in a cultural ideal, as well as exclusion from it, can do damage. Simultaneously, stories of aging out of authorship bolster the narrative authority of white adults, such as Carmen's teacher-editor, Mirthes. Wordsworth and his contemporaries invoke nostalgia for lost childhood as a key component of the adult author's construction of a poetic self. The literary voice is figured partly through the performance of mourning for childhood's "unrecoverability."[12] Whereas Wordsworth mourns his own lost childhood, twentieth-century teacher-editors like Mirthes lament the maturation of their former students. The resulting narratives boost adult teacher-editors' textual charisma at the expense of the no-longer-child authors being mourned. As important as it is, then, to "acknowledg[e] that young people can be artists or poets in the present, now, *while* they are young," as Conrad advocates, we must also reckon with destructive idealizations of child writers.[13] Our best guides to understanding and advancing alternatives to such narratives are young writers themselves.

This chapter argues that classroom-based child authors craft temporal tactics to critique and negotiate the time-telling forces of public education, classroom literary production, and anthology publication. Young writers use adult-controlled literary opportunities to engage the highly time-bound ways in which they are moved through the school system, cultivated as writers, published, and read. Confronting the centrality of temporal regimes to the pathologization, criminalization, and control of Black and Puerto Rican children, classroom writers script their own rhythms, shaping alternative choreographies of time and possibility. Queer theorists of childhood have examined the temporal structure of childhood and its implications for equity and justice, while critics have noted young writers' affinity for temporal plays. Building on Rachel Conrad's account of young writers' "temporal agency," I apply an intersectional view of childhood temporality, arguing for young writers' engagements with the racial politics of time and age.[14]

Carmen and her peers contribute to a long tradition of anti-racist temporal practice. As Michael Hanchard has argued, through "racial time," the pervasive use of temporal inequalities and disjunctures has been a key structural element of racist power. African American liberation struggles have thus developed tools of "time appropriation, seizing another's time and making it one's own." Citing Black Panther Party cofounder Bobby Seale's call to "seize the time," Hanchard locates a "need to appropriate a new temporality, wherein new values, freedoms, and forms of expression are operative."[15] African American literature has been a consistently potent site of anti-racist temporality, as Daylanne English demonstrates. English cites eighteenth-century child poet Phillis Wheatley as an early practitioner of tracking the temporal manifestations of power and "challeng[ing] an abstractly universalized time."[16] Joining this project, Carmen and her peers apply their specific temporal position as racially and socioeconomically marginalized schoolchildren in order to craft literary contestations of "racial time." By challenging the dominating processes of time-telling, classroom writers align themselves with the critique by Martin Luther King, Jr., of liberal white efforts to dictate the timing of black freedom struggle. Children confront the future as a potential space of domination, as well as liberation, thus surfacing the complexity of temporal struggle. Circa-1970 young writers respond to King's counsel that "we must use time creatively, in the knowledge that the time is always ripe to do right."[17]

In particular, I argue, young writers challenge and evade time-telling with their own preemptive practices. Children predict, overleap, and anticipate what is to come, in a strategy resonant with Margo Natalie Crawford's concept of anticipatory aesthetics during and after the Black Arts Movement. "Black anticipatory aesthetics is the art of not knowing what blackness will be; it is the art situated within the sustained dissonance of the earlier chords being heard, simultaneously, with the sounds that are just beginning to emerge," Crawford writes.[18] Crawford emphasizes the anticipation of positive possibility, whereas I find that young writers often anticipate threats as well as dreams of the future. Still, children's anticipatory styles evince a strong link to the aesthetics examined by Crawford, as young writers craft temporal styles in connection and in conversation with the broader Black Arts Movement.

I consider authors from two classroom anthologies: the troublingly structured *Can't You Hear Me Talking to You?* and a more child-shaped collection, *The Children: Poems and Prose from Bedford-Stuyvesant*. The children that contributed to these volumes engaged with their teachers in tense yet collaborative processes of representing childhood, generating highly time-conscious literary forms. Classroom writers' engagements with narrative time intervene in a cross-age conversation about the ways in which marginalized children's stories should be told.

TEMPORAL LOGICS IN THE SCHOOL SYSTEM AND BOOK PUBLICATION

Circa-1970 classroom writing developed within public schooling's highly timed system of knowledge and control. The US school system advances an ideal of temporal lockstep—that every child progresses at the same rate, along the same curricular and developmental schedule—despite evidence to the contrary. Lawmakers have articulated this principle in initiatives from Head Start (1965) to No Child Left Behind (2001). These federal program titles conjure the threatening reality of their negative: children delayed and behind. The school ideal of temporal lockstep structures a system that, in reality, operates not by progressing everyone together but rather through "holding back," "repeating," "detention," "suspension": even school punishment is temporal, as it is also carceral. The elaborate metrics of testing and tracking that have been worked and reworked since the 1960s, claiming to measure which children are learning at what rate, both respond to and reinforce the gap between the ideal of lockstep progress and the uneven, unequal American reality.

The absurdities resulting from this ideal caught the attention of 1960s–1970s anti-racist thinkers. David Perez centers a critique of the US school system within the Young Lords' anticolonial framework. Perez analyzes US schooling as a form of "cultural genocide": "In the school system here [in the US mainland], if you don't quickly begin to speak English and shed your Puerto Rican values, you're put back a grade—so you may be in the sixth grade in Puerto Rico but when you come here, you go back to the fourth or fifth. You're treated as if you're retarded, as if you're backward." [19] As demonstrated by the Young Lords, many of whom were still in youth themselves, school temporalities played a central, illustrative role in the era's radical political analyses of US white supremacy and imperialism. Resonant with Perez's commentary, Jonathan Kozol's book *Death at an Early Age* describes the reading materials available during his time teaching at a de facto segregated Black school in Boston in the 1960s. The school's stock of extremely old, out-of-date textbooks ironically promoted a narrative of white American progress. Kozol implicitly links textbook expiration to his titular concept of childhood death, whether literal or social. [20]

Teacher-editors of Mirthes's era largely saw themselves as aligned with Kozol, against the racist, stiflingly conventional institution of public education. They conceived of classroom anthologies as using the power of children's voices to expose and attack a fundamentally broken school system. In their deep distrust of the school system and the majority of its teachers, teacher-editors understandably sought to fend off what they saw as the near-inevitable destruction of their students' futures. These educators' narrative devices, however, risk reproducing the temporal tendencies of that very system. Teacher-editors tend to portray their classrooms as ephemeral utopias, from which students must ultimately be ejected back into the cruel, corrupting world. The prevalence of class anthologies from the sixth grade, usually the last year of elementary school in this era, enhances this sense of loss. [21] Come June and junior high, the books imply, students fall out of the utopian classroom, out of innocence—and out of childhood.

Teachers' efforts to protect space for children's learning and self-expression can effectively freeze them in the time and space of that class, eliding children's ongoing creative lives. Child authors remain static, preserved on the ice of elegy, while teacher-editors move forward with the process of marketing, printing, and profiting from classroom writings. This process can occur in the very act of asserting children's present-day relevance, as demonstrated by Mirthes: "They [her students] are not a 'problem' that can be dealt with in a year, or ten years from now, but twelve- and thirteen-year-olds *whose chances for life have changed even in the time it has taken to prepare and publish this book.*"[22] Even in the mode of child advocacy, the freezing of young writers' childhood operates in tandem with the processes of adult publication. The time-bound nature of public school classes, translated into the language of book sales, shapes narratives of literary childhood in ephemeral and elegiac terms. This kind of storytelling forecloses writers' post-classroom lives, disqualifying them not only from childhood but also from authorial status, as if writers had no ability to extend creative production beyond this timeline. Child authorship becomes a narrow window of possibility, the foreclosure of which is central to the genre's appeal. Classroom anthologies thus betray adults' tendency to age children out of authorship.

As the texts discussed in this chapter reveal, child writers observed and contested this temporal logic. In the process, they advanced the radical movement for educational racial justice in late 1960s and early 1970s America. Historical accounts of the era's school justice battles have illuminated the work of adult leaders, such as the Reverend Milton Galamison and the educator and activist Jitu Weusi (Leslie Campbell).[23] We have much to learn about children's active roles in such phenomena as the community control movement, beyond their place as symbolic figures or victims of education disputes. This chapter presents classroom-based writers, particularly girls, as creative and intellectual contributors to 1960s–1970s educational radicalism and challengers of the dominant order of public school.

CARMEN'S TEMPORAL TACTICS OF SURVIVAL

Carmen's self-dating in "You've Got to Fight the Right Way" plays with the calendar structure of schooling. She puts a twist on "Name and Date," that dutiful double headline of school compositions drilled into students' heads. In addition to falling a month after King's assassination, Carmen's date sits

squarely within the New York school year. But May 4, 1968, was also a Saturday, subtly marking the writer's autonomy from the physical space and time
of the classroom.

Even as Carmen sets the time frame of her own text, "You've Got to Fight
the Right Way" acquires an additional explanatory apparatus within its
teacher-edited publication. Mirthes prefaces Carmen's essay, like many of
the anthology texts, with psychologizing backstory. Over spring vacation,
Mirthes divulges, Carmen was badly injured while defending her young
brother in a fight, only to be scorned by her mother for losing. Carmen
"called me up, her voice trembling," Mirthes states, and the two "talked for
almost an hour" about Carmen's mother and Carmen's own life choices.
"When she returned to school a week later, she presented me with this
essay."[24] Mirthes shapes an interpretation of the essay by retemporalizing
it. Her focus on time—"[d]uring spring vacation," "for almost an hour," "a
week later"—positions the essay at the endpoint of a neat narrative arc that
lacks any reference to King's death. The story begins with Carmen's fights
in the street and at home, turns with Mirthes's phone conversation, and
triumphantly concludes not with Carmen's writing of the essay but with its
receipt in Mirthes's hands. The teacher-editor inserts herself as a character and even coauthor of Carmen's text, which does not itself mention her
teacher.

Carmen's authorial self-presentation and Mirthes's explanation mark
divergent ways of conceptualizing child authorship. Carmen's essay leaves
the idea of "fighting right" elusive, providing more exhortation than explanation. The writer implies that *you*, the reader, "must fight with your brain,"
engage in intellectual struggle in order to understand Carmen's ideas.
"[A]nd you have got to know how to do it": reading, like fighting, can be
done wrong and requires skill. Mirthes's framing, in contrast, portrays
the essay as symptomatic of events in Carmen's life and world, specifically
Carmen's Lower East Side neighborhood as it is raced and classed as a site
of violence, social dysfunction, and family neglect. By presenting herself
as a necessary interpreter, Mirthes implicitly classifies children's writing
as *to-be-explained*.[25] This label denotes the shunting of children's writings
simultaneously into the future and the past. Adult-controlled processes of
explanation and interpretation can suggest that children's writing acquires
meaning only in the future, beyond the timeframe of children's composition. Here the parental platitude "You'll understand when you're older"

becomes applicable even to children's own literary work. The frequent reliance of adult explanations on discourses of poverty pathology, meanwhile, tends to figure marginalized children's writings as the inevitable product of their social conditions, shutting the book on children's meanings as always already past tense.

In response to this threat, Carmen's writings provide a guide and antidote to the dangers of time-telling. In two essays that, in Mirthes's words, "became classics in the school" among students, Carmen adapts the conventionally scholastic five-paragraph essay form to address young people's survival in the "slums," her term for deeply impoverished and oppressed New York neighborhoods.[26] Compact and focused, titled with catchy slogans, "You've Got to Fight the Right Way" and "How Does a Block Swallowed You Up" are designed for popular circulation. As the former essay fights right by setting its own timeline and refusing full explicability, the latter provides instruction in discerning and evading temporal control.

"How Does a Block Swallowed You Up" addresses a seemingly unavoidable system of peer manipulation. Carmen warns her peers of the dangers of the slums, specifically from other young people who, in Carmen's words, "want you to be like one more victim of their block" through social entanglement, violence, and drug use. The essay promises a way for kids to avoid learning lessons "the hard way": that is, Carmen's essay aims to reach her readers preemptively, before danger does.[27]

Carmen portrays peer threat as primarily a matter of words. She describes an intricate choreography of telling, saying, and asking through which peers entangle newcomers. The game begins with a false show of friendliness: "They tell you their names. . . . Then they ask you how old are you and they ask you that before they tell you their age because they want to make themselves older than you." This friendly dialogue then shifts to baiting for a fight: "That is the conversation that could make the block swallowed you." Physical threat here reinforces the primary tactic of verbal manipulation. The danger here is *conversation*, a maze of words with all exits verbally blocked off: "Well the conversation starts like this first they tell you you're a nice friend. You know then they tell you do you know how to fight . . . all of a sudden they tell you you're cheating [at a game] . . . you say I wasn't cheating. But they always receive the same excuse so they already have an answer to that. Then they tell you don't you call me a liar." These tactics corner the newcomer into fighting, then facing escalating dares to take drugs. The bullies dictate an apparently airtight causal chain, so that one act inescapably leads to the next. A denial of cheating leads to a physical fight, puffing a cigarette to sniffing glue. Carmen's narration reenacts that process, telling the reader what "you" undoubtedly think, feel, and do: "Then you certainly wouldn't want to start up so you say I wasn't cheating. . . . Then the worst thing comes to your head and you push back."[28] The second person brings the described sequence into the real time of reading, so that the reader experiences the claustrophobic merging of pressured present and dictated future. The repeated conjunctive adverb *then* encapsulates the temporal takeover of this controlling logic of inevitability. Carmen's performative imitation of the bullies reveals peer manipulation as a form of narrative, which denies a young person's ability to make choices and determine her own story by rendering her identity and future already explained.

Carmen's essay takes on the fear of becoming the mere product of one's environment, "like one more victim of their block." Her eight repetitions of the clause "they tell you" gradually shift from simply referring to dialogue to implying commands, as in *they tell you what to do*. Telling you what to do, here, also implies *telling you what you are*. The local threat of kid bullies reflects the broader threat of racist national discourses of poverty pathology, which construct poor children of color as the dangerous products of dysfunctional neighborhoods. As Carmen repeats the bullies' pronoun, *they*, it acquires a secondary signification as an adult societal *they*, who tell particular age-, race-, class- and gender-based stories about the lives of Carmen and her peers. The clause "they tell you" evokes the tellings of teachers and social workers, newspapers and TV, juvenile courts and presidential administrations: *they* who, throughout the 1960s, articulated the problem of children's urban poverty not in the language of justice but in the language of threat. *They* often drew on such rhetoric in their very advocacy for children, as demonstrated by the 1965 proposal for the Head Start program: "For the child of poverty there are clearly observable deficiencies in the processes which lay the foundation for a pattern of failure—and thus a pattern of poverty—throughout the child's entire life."[29] By taking on time-telling on the block, then, Carmen also addresses this process on the scale of the nation.

Carmen illustrates her temporal battle through the structuring metaphor of being swallowed. The essay concludes: "So be a hero like I'm trying to be.

Don't let a block swallowed you. Please swallow all the blocks you can but don't let them get you. You won't like it. Good Bye."[30] The oral image emphasizes danger as conversational, a matter of the tongue. Carmen's use of *swallowed* in the grammatical place of *swallow* deems the event foregone even at the time of warning. The past participle threatens to "swallowed" any present or future possibilities, as if one's fate is always already told. This hint of past tense also reflects the extent to which Carmen's metaphor and essay are about loss, the irrevocability of decisions and the irretrievability of childhood years.

Complete with a memorable moral, the dramatic end to the essay nevertheless offers only tentative resolution to its articulated threat. In comparison with the blow-by-blow description of the problem, the solution remains abstract and brief, occupying only the last fraction of the final paragraph. Carmen stops short of concretely explaining how "a kid that is good" can "swallow all the blocks you can." Her plan for resistance remains as indigestible as the thought of consuming a city block, crunching with brick and glass. The problem of the essay thus threatens to "swallowed" up its solution. A disquieting weighting of words toward the problem, rather than the solution, characterizes "You've Got to Fight the Right Way," as well as "How Does a Block," perverting the problem-solution structure of the scholastic five-paragraph essay. This evasion of full explicability unsettles assumptions of a neat beginning, middle, and end. Denying the representation of children of color as fully explainable and predictable, Carmen's texts counteract the dominating tell-all style deployed by Mirthes, the bullies on the block, and broader juvenile delinquency discourse.

With her own escape from swallowing veiled in reticence, Carmen leaves readers with data on only one of her tactics, that of essay-writing itself. Her literary production is an act of swallowing, a capacious means to take in one's own surroundings and conditions. Moreover, her success in circulating the essays, both throughout her school and later in the published anthology, suggests a power of extension beyond the narrow lockdown of a block. Mirthes's preface to "How Does a Block" plays into this contrast: "[Carmen] laughed and bent down and pulled from her knee socks six pages of the following composition. She had locked herself in the bathroom to write it and then hidden it so her parents wouldn't see it."[31] Mirthes's anecdote projects a certain cuteness onto the essay, while also positioning herself as the agent of literary release. But the claustrophobia of the locked bathroom and the knee sock, followed by the release of the pages and of Carmen's laughter, evokes the expansiveness required to "swallow all the blocks you can." This sense of unbounded dispersal resonates with the ways in which Carmen's text withholds clarity and resolution. The force of Carmen's essay lies partly in the persistent puzzle of its slogan, the fugitive nature of what exactly it would mean to "swallow all the blocks you can."

The writer's logic remains difficult to swallow(ed), her life sticking in the throat as incompletely told. In this way, Carmen responds to the particular risks of classroom-based literary production. By collaborating with Mirthes, Carmen gained a broader audience and resources but also embedded her literary work within the time-telling structures of the racialized school system, which threatened to erase young people's possibilities and age children out of authorship. Carmen presciently counteracts this threat of scholastic swallowing by equipping her texts, and thus their peer readers, with the rhetorical tools to confound the logic of pathology and tell one's own time.

YOLANDA PRESCOTT'S DETOURS OF POSSIBILITY

Across the East River, Brooklyn student Yolanda Prescott crafted her own temporal challenge. Ten-year-old Prescott (published as Yolanda McDade) contributed her story "The Storm" to *The Children: Poems and Prose from Bedford-Stuyvesant*, edited by Irving Benig, a novelist and playwright who taught in the Brooklyn neighborhood of Bedford-Stuyvesant as a legal alternative to the Vietnam War draft. Benig's students, most of whom remained in his class for two years, garnered broad attention for their writings, appearing on *Good Morning America* and the *David Frost Show* (fig. 3). In "The Storm," Prescott brings the temporal argument expressed in Carmen's work into an affectively and stylistically distinct form of "fighting right," lit by joyful wandering and magical opportunity. Prescott's meditation on simultaneity and possibility dissolves the airtight causal logic of time-telling.[32]

Signaling its pressure on preexisting terms of childhood possibility, the story opens with two acts of pushing: "While sitting inside watching the rain the window was pushed against by a teenager by the name of Tarina Summers. She pushed the rocking chair up against the wall and saw a stray cat walking across the Patcher's patio."[33] Tarina physically modifies the

FIGURE 3. Authors of *The Children: Poems and Prose from Bedford-Stuyvesant* in class with Irving Benig (standing at back), circa 1970. —Courtesy of Irving Benig.

insulating setting given to her. Her gestures set in place the driving motive for the story, perhaps inspired by the sight of the strolling cat: a desire for direct contact with the rain. The "name of Tarina Summers," presented rather grandly in the story's first sentence, holds meaning beyond its status as a cherished fantasy identity. *Tarina* is a semi-anagram of *rain*, and *Summers* alludes to both the season of summer, or freedom from school, and the repetition of that season over the years. The juxtaposition of these first and last names suggests the temporal flavor of the storm, a larger-than-life, cyclically created force that temporarily transforms interludes of human experience. This process of transitory transformation shapes Prescott's narrative.

In a magic window of adult-free time, Tarina's aloneness and consequent meditative monologue establish the enchantment of the story. "She said to herself, 'Since my mother isn't going to come home until it stops raining I know what I should do. I should take my bike and ride it in the rain.'" This idea launches a vividly unclear reflection on possibility: "Oh what beautiful

rainbows I would see laying in the streets. Sometimes I would once be able
to pick it up but I know it's impossible."[34] This statement could be taken
pragmatically to mean, *I used to think I could pick up rainbows but now I know
better.* The syntax, however, indicates something closer to, *Sometimes I know
that/will that I'll be able to pick up a rainbow, even though it's impossible.* The
ambiguity here stems partly from the double temporal significance of the
verb *would*, which can serve as either a future conditional or the imperfect
past tense. Tarina's *would* suggests both her anticipation of going outside and
her memory of how things used to be. In this way, the narration moves in two
temporal directions, impressionistically blurring the line between practical
and magical thinking. The story leaves a sense of a girl's growing up, developing firmer ideas of what is possible and reasonable, yet retaining the residues
of imagination and desires from her younger childhood. Tarina's *would* also
suggests the double meaning of *will*, denoting individual decision making
and drive. Suspending the impossible across verb tense and aspect, Prescott
portrays the practice of carving out personal freedom from the very material
of time, both in experience and in narrative.

Prescott's atmospheric prose layers multiple planes of time. The description of Tarina's biking pleasure exemplifies this effect. "The thunder started
rolling across the grey and white sky. As it started Tarina sped down Maple
St. As she did she still saw her rocking chair still rocking back and forth and
the stray cat still walking across the Patcher's patio."[35] Time words like *started,
as,* and *still* suggest the writer's investment in conjuring multiple, overlapping
temporal trajectories. Rolling thunder, speeding Tarina, rocking chair, and
pacing cat each follow an individual rhythm, as if populating a world with
variously ticking clocks. The second glimpse of the cat's stroll here exemplifies the writer's use of peripheral glimpses to cultivate a sense of a larger
world happening around Tarina. Ripples of movement and stillness, stasis
and change, evoke a plurality and simultaneity of being. The cat will keep
walking and the chair will keep rocking even after passing out of Tarina's and
the reader's view.

Time catches up to Tarina in the figure of her mother. "As she turned on
Dextin Ave. she saw her mother and turned the bike around but then heard
her mother's voice, 'Tarina, Tarina Summers.' Her mother ran down Dextin
Ave." Tarina's attempt to rewind comes too late: her mother has returned
earlier than promised, while rain still falls, and caught Tarina in the act. The
mother sharply halts the dreamy course of the story: "As she [the mother]

approached her she looked at her face and it was red and hot! 'It's that way because you forgot about your hat, raincoat and boots. Why? Why, Tarina Summers? Your father will hear about this.'"[36] There is the sense that Tarina's face grows hot only when caught. If a chair rocks in an empty house, does it still creak, and if a girl bikes coatless in the rain without her parents' knowing, does she still catch a fever? The mother's pronouncement, "It's that way because," strikes like lightning or illness, delivering relentlessly causal logic: *if coatless in the rain, then sick*. Her form of storytelling advances a rigidly causal understanding of time, by which each event inevitably leads to the next. In seeking to explain reality, this kind of telling also makes a reality, as the mother's words cue Tarina's fever.

Despite this imposition of certainty, the mother opens up her own field of possibilities. Her unexpectedly early return suggests her own untold, unpredictable story taking place out of view, her own tussle with time for work, responsibilities, or freedom. By appearing out of turn, the mother's character seems to refuse the narrative bounds set by protagonist Tarina or author Prescott. The mother's question, moreover—"Why? Why, Tarina Summers?"—opens the way for Tarina's own reasoning to have the last word in the narrative. The last lines of the story offer an intergenerational dialogue of temporal perspectives as a kind of consolation prize for the fevered ending of Tarina's ride. Her concluding line constitutes the only thought in the story that Tarina speaks to someone besides herself: "I just wanted to feel the coolness break through me."[37] This statement of desire suggests an alternate logic to adults' unbending causality. Tarina names a dream of being literally in touch with one's environment and allowing oneself to be acted on and through, not as an inevitable, passive product of environmental conditions but as one whose openness to exposure and possibility moves toward transcendence, "breaking through" one's body and perhaps even one's own identity. "The Storm" refracts threatening narratives of inevitability through a mist of possibility, asserting a young writer's mobility through plural, multidirectional streams of time.

More than fifty years later, Prescott is a lifelong poet as well as an educator, social worker, church elder, youth minister, and soon-to-be children's book author. Prescott reflects on her early years of writing in Benig's class: "When it would rain in Brooklyn, I would crack open the window and just look out. Writing provided me an escape to personal pains I experienced in my own home. Daydreaming allowed me to create characters like Tarina and . . . be someplace other than where I was. Mr. Benig taught me how to write stories and escape. And Escape I did! He was the vessel I needed and he did not know it. My classmates and I were the vessels he needed to fight the Vietnam War in Bed-Stuy. We needed each other. And for this I am forever grateful. We survived the war."[38]

"TALKING ABOUT THEMSELVES": DEIDRE HARRIS'S USABLE PAST

A classmate of Prescott and fellow contributor to *The Children*, nine-year-old Deidre Harris, opens her historical play *Slavery Escape* with three layers of dialogue:

> NOAH: Our story begins when Mr. Hadfield and Mr. D. J.
>   Macould are discussing their slaves. As the men talk,
>   Harriet says to the others:
> HARRIET: There are two things we have a right to, even if we are
>   slaves, and that is death and liberty.[39]

While the slaveholders discuss where to put their captives to work for the day, four enslaved companions begin a conversation about their rights. Straddling these two conversations, Noah, who is both a character and the narrator of the play, generates a third level of dialogue, explicitly directed to the audience. In line with Prescott, Harris generates a sense of simultaneity, in which multiple experiences and perspectives spread through a single narrative of time. In the case of *Slavery Escape*, this overlapping strengthens the ability of historical drama to perform the past into coexistence with the present. *Slavery Escape* unfolds two timelines, both the explicit plotline of the captive characters' self-liberation and the implicit historical trajectory from the antebellum dramatic setting to the writer's late 1960s America. This doubling shapes the play's complex engagements with the passage of time.

The plot of *Slavery Escape* emphasizes the gradual unfolding of self-liberation across the fabric of time. Harriet's opening gambit begins this process, spurring a collective endeavor of interpretation among her friends.

> HARRIET: There are two things we have a right to, even if we
>   are slaves, and that is death and liberty.
> FREDERICK: What exactly do you mean, Harriet?
> HARRIET: I don't exactly know how to put it.

. . . .

MARY: I can't help thinking what Harriet meant.
FREDERICK: I think Harriet knows what she's doing. You don't
have to have an education to know that.

. . . .

NOAH: Now it is night and slaves are talking about themselves.
HARRIET: Now I will tell you what I meant this afternoon. I
meant we must escape.
NOAH: They all shouted, "What, escape?"[40]

The three moments above, spread over the course of a day in the enslaved life of four intimates, portray the development of individual and collective thought. The friends work to refine and articulate their ideas, confronting ambiguity and difficulty: "I don't know exactly how to put it. . . . I can't help thinking what Harriet meant." The characters thus model for audiences the process of slow, thoughtful reading. In line with this metaliterary dimension, group leader Harriet's name aligns her not only with Harriet Tubman but also with play-wright Harris. The presence of Noah as combined character-narrator further enhances textual self-consciousness. As he puts it, under cover of night, "slaves are talking about themselves," rather than simply talking *among* themselves and rather than solely *being* discussed by Hadfield and Macould. By evening, punc-tuated by the repetition of *now*—"Now it is night. . . . Now I will tell you"—the group has readied itself to confront Harriet's bold proposal.

Harris's focus on the drama of intellectual exchange may explain the apparent temporal eccentricities of her plot. Harriet shares her plan for the friends to stow away to freedom on a wagon of corn, hopping off into a ditch and then walking to the "master's town," where the group can live free. The group's enactment of the plan fails when they are spotted by the wagon-driver, returned to the slaveholders, and punished with whippings. Harriet soon convinces the group to "try again," and according to Noah's narration, "this time they had a better plan than ever." But in fact, the plotters "meet at the same place"; "her plan was the same plan." Once again, the fugitives hide in the corn wagon before jumping in the ditch, but this time with success. Noah's report that the second plan was "better . . . than ever" yet somehow exactly "the same" indicates that the improvement lies in the group's understanding.

Noah concludes the script: "They walked a mile and came to master's town and Harriet shouted, 'FREEDOM AT LAST!' She and Frederick settled down in a four room little house and Noah married Mary."[41] The brevity of escape and abruptness of success, punctuated by Harriet's capitalized shout and sealed with a conventionally marital happy ending, stands in contrast to the sober deliberations and iterations of the play's first half.

Harris's theatrical shaping of time resonates with Black radical conceptions of the interconnections of past, present, and future. Her repeated use of the word *now* to move along the action of the play echoes both civil rights calls for "freedom now" and Black Power visions of liberation in Harris's time. Harriet's abrupt and pointed declaration "FREEDOM AT LAST!" continues this political trope of refusing to wait. The relative physical and logistical ease of flight, in which the playwright seems minimally interested, suggests that the most salient challenge is mental, the collective work of thought and conversation for liberation. Hanchard notes: "Temporal freedom meant not only an abolition of the temporal constraints slave labor placed on New World Africans but also the freedom to construct individual and collective temporality that existed autonomously from (albeit contemporaneously with) the temporality of their former masters."[42] By enacting a happy ending of escape in the space of historical drama, Harris pulls the futurity of the past into the present. In conversation with the era's growing genre of neo-slave narratives, Harris's play contributes to Black Arts efforts to generate a recuperative counternarrative of the past that supports the enactment of Nation Time in the future-realizing present.[43]

The implausibility of Harris's escape plot, in contrast to her generally impressive historical fidelity, may also point to a note of irony. Growing up in de facto segregation in 1960s Brooklyn, the playwright would have known well the limited happy endings available in Freedom North. Her repeated reference to the site of freedom as "master's town" and its short distance from enslavement—a mile would barely take the writer out of Bedford-Stuyvesant—hints that Harriet, Frederick, Noah, and Mary may find their new home less than liberatory. The dubious moniker "master's town" could also satirize the conventional assumption, rebutted by anti-racist and decolonial movements, that the oppressed seek nothing more than the lifestyle of their oppressors. Even as the play seems to embrace conventional narrative closure, its perfunctory happy ending invites doubt.

In light of this ambiguity, the initial expression of astonishment from Harriet's friends—"What, escape?"—can also be read as an actual question, an interrogation of the contours of *escape* as a concept and a tactic. The humor here partly lies in the obviousness of the idea of escaping slavery from the retrospective view of Harris's time; the play imagines a moment before the mythologization of Harriet Tubman. It is easy to imagine the comma in this scripted line being added by an adult, raising the possibility of a more directly questioning response: "What escape?" This query draws an implicit parallel to the teleologies of escape surrounding marginalized child writers.

Children sometimes framed their writing in the terms of flight, as Prescott's recollection demonstrates: "And escape I did!" The trope of escape was complicated by the tendency of white adult discourse to figure neighborhoods like the Lower East Side and Bedford-Stuyvesant as places to be fled, specifically by educationally successful children. Caroline Mirthes presents her anthology itself as a means of such evasion:

> I have thought of this book as an extended plea for help for the children who have written with such insight, and who have already survived so much. It was my dream that they could go to boarding school on scholarship—and that they would grow and flourish in a more peaceful atmosphere.... It has been arranged that any profits from this book will go directly into a fund for the further education of the children whose essays we have included.[44]

Mirthes was not alone in seeking new school arrangements for her students: the adult directors of the Voice of the Children, June Jordan and Terri Bush, also made efforts to secure private school admissions and scholarships for some young writers.[45] Mirthes's dream of her students' flight into privilege, however, acknowledges young writers' real suffering at the cost of reifying the construction of their families and neighborhoods as sites of foreclosure. In his own anthology preface, Irving Benig more ironically engages this discourse of escape, wryly repeating the common characterization of "'bad' area[s] ... where blacks and Puerto Ricans ruined teachers, robbed stores, and killed each other." Benig discloses that he took advantage of a policy by which teaching in such a "bad area" exempted him from a bigger danger, the Vietnam War draft. This teaching opportunity "was a sweet sanctuary into which we scurried. I can only say that, for myself, I took it as the only gambit given to me if I did not want to exile myself as my grandfather had, long ago in another time, when he came to America from Russia to avoid compulsory military conscription."[46] Benig ties the conditions of Bedford-Stuyvesant to US intervention in Vietnam, which several of his students' texts protest. His personal confession unsettles the concepts of escape and sanctuary central to the conventional American dream. It is the perceived desolation of Bedford-Stuyvesant, its figuration as a place to be escaped, that allows it to serve as a sanctuary for Benig. Benig's students, meanwhile, are the descendants of generations of migrations to Brooklyn, including many African Americans fleeing the South. Teachers and students might provide each other with sanctuary, as Prescott's adult recollection suggests: "We needed each other." The writing classroom could thus serve as a space of teacher-student mutuality, in which children and adults could aid each other's dreams of elsewhere while also thinking through the complexities and limitations of escape as a concept. Variously registering the association of child authorship with teleologies of escape, Mirthes, Benig, and Prescott surface the contemporary significance of Harris's critical question: "What, escape?"[47]

In this mode of transhistorical connection, Harris's drama both invites and complicates the allegory between antebellum enslavement and circa-1970 schooling. The language of modern classroom interactions infuses *Slavery Escape.* The setup of the opening scene, with two "Mr." authorities discussing their charges as they whisper among themselves, resembles the hierarchical arrangement of a classroom. Mr. Hadfield interrupts the slaves' discussion in the field with a perfect imitation of a twentieth-century schoolteacher: "A little more work and less talking!"[48] In contrasting moments, the escaping friends conduct their own scenes of instruction. While Harriet most obviously educates the group by introducing new ideas, spurring conversation, and giving directives, additional characters variously adopt a teacherly stance. Frederick's response to her initial proposal, for instance—"What exactly do you mean, Harriet?"—channels a teacher's probing for precise expression. Through a plurality of teacherly figures, the play asks what kinds of teaching and learning support liberation, evoking 1960s–1970s experimental, community-based education. Frederick's later remark to Mary, "You don't have to have an education to know that," echoes Black Power thinkers' commitment to nontraditional learning and extracurricular knowledge.[49] Harris thus provides an incomplete, contradictory allegory between historical slavery and the writer's public school classroom. The past and present connect, she suggests, through nonlinear resonances rather than one-to-one correspondence or simple arcs of progress. She leaves open the questions of whether schoolteachers are enemies or collaborators and whether classroom writing may be exploitative labor demanded by authoritative misters or a collective act of liberation. Playfully drawing on scholastic culture, Harris stages young writers' "talking about themselves" both within and beyond the bounded time, space, and social order of the classroom.

By dramatizing the intellectual work of communal change, Harris joins Black Arts playwrights' use of theater to imagine and enact conceptual struggles for political consciousness.[50] Emphasizing the iterative, ongoing nature of liberation through time, troubling teleologies of escape, and tangling allegory, *Slavery Escape* portrays meaning as a continually unfolding, interpersonal process. As Carmen combats time-telling and evades explicability and Prescott charts possibility outside narratives of inevitability, Harris's temporal doublings, loops, and knots scramble the forms of storytelling that impose finalizing explanation on marginalized children's creative lives. These writers demonstrate the array of genres, tones, and rhetorical techniques that classroom writers deploy to interrogate and reshape children's positions in time.

A QUESTION OF "INTENT": TIME IN THE ARCHIVES OF *THE CHILDREN*

Classroom writers' temporal tactics prompt attention to the politics of time and sequence within processes of publishing children's writings. Following the leads of Carmen, Prescott, and Harris, I conduct a time-based scrutiny of one particularly well-documented publication process, Irving Benig's work with Grove Press to release *The Children: Poems and Prose from Bedford-Stuyvesant*. Archival documents from the press, including Benig's correspondence with his editor at Grove, Marilyn Meeker, register the clash of rhythms at work in the negotiation of children's authorial rights and editorial control.

Benig's first pitch to Grove, penned in a hand as bold as his words, straddles two views of child writers: as passive sources of material and as real-time coauthors. In this initial attempt to tell a story about his classroom, Benig simultaneously markets his individual achievement and the collective literary labors of his student writers.

> Dear Miss Meeker:
>
> I have an idea for a book you will be interested in. I also have the book. I am a teacher. I've gotten thirty-two children in Bedford-Stuyvesant to write 38 pages of brilliant, witty and cool poems, letters and essays. One of them illustrated these pages. I think it is precisely the kind of material which is the genesis of a remarkable book. If you give me an appointment, I will bring the MSS and convince you.
>
> Awaiting,
>
> Irving Benig[51]

Benig's brazenly repeated *I*, the subject of all but one sentence of the letter, centers himself as the white adult male authorial entity for sale. The casually forceful term *gotten* credits Benig himself with the literary production of his students, who are implicitly raced and classed through the label of "Bedford-Stuyvesant." *I've* and *gotten*, as in *having* and *getting*, suggest possession, with past participles reminiscent of Carmen's "swallowed." Benig implies that as he has "gotten" his students to write brilliantly, so he "will . . . convince" the editor, without question.

Counterbalancing Benig's few sentences of self-promotion, however, is the bulk of the children's "38 pages." Characterized by three adjectives and three nouns—"brilliant, witty and cool poems, letters and essays"—the children's writings give the pitch its center of gravity. Benig's description of these writings momentarily breaks the first-person hold of his letter to allow a sentence with a child subject: "One of them illustrated these pages." The confluence of Benig's personal act of *getting* with the children's collective acts of *writing* and *illustrating* shapes an enticingly double conception of authorship in Benig's class collection.

Benig uses this complexity of literary production to make temporal arguments for his potential book. He portrays himself and his students' work as ahead of the curve. Not only does he "have an idea" that Meeker certainly "*will* be interested in" (italics mine), but "I also have the book." The second sentence leapfrogs ahead of the first, positioning the book as fresher than fresh. In this way, Benig performs in response to Grove's reputation for "aesthetic daring, shocking content, unique or 'avant-garde' textual practices, or at the very least titillating good times."[52] He suggests that these qualities reside both in the children's writings and in his own self-consciously youthful persona, riding the cutting edge while impatiently "awaiting" Grove editors to catch up.

In line with his first-person sell, Benig repeatedly bids for an in-person presentation of the book material to Meeker, rather than continuing correspondence. To his first promise to "bring the MSS and convince you," Meeker coolly responds, "As you know there are a number of [similar] books on the market, however, if you wish to send us the manuscript, we will be glad to read it." In response to the implication that he is late to the party, Benig mails some of the children's work, with the caveat that "I have a vision of the book, but, alas! only in my mind's eye. Give me an appointment . . ."[53] Benig and Meeker here tussle over sequence: he proposes to meet and then convince her, while she insists on being convinced before meeting. Benig unsuccessfully seeks what child writers rarely secure: the ability to move with one's text, to oversee its circulation and reception in real time. To enhance the allure of his pitch, Benig works to maintain his presentation of the book as both fait accompli and future promise, deliberately muddling the issue of whether or not a manuscript yet exists. This temporal question, moreover, depends on conceptions of authorship: if the children have generated their texts but the book exists only in a teacher-editor's "mind's eye," then the children must not be its primary authors.

Benig's self-positioning as real-time and ahead-of-time depends on maneuvers around children's past, present, and future. To Meeker's suggestion that similar books are already out, Benig provides six reasons why his project is newer and better:

1. unlike similar books, this one is written by the pupils of only one class
2. unlike similar books, not one piece in this book is by a child over twelve
3. the literary quality of this book is far above those of similar content
4. the book will be illustrated by Randy Cook, age 11, whose samplings can be seen on the cover enclosed (Randy has already won a scholarship to Pratt Institute)
5. the book will have a political and social impact far out of proportion to its intent
6. it will make money[54]

Benig's rationale links "literary quality" to limitations on literary production: the constrained space and time of "only one class"—a model less unique than he claims—and the related age cap of "not one piece . . . by a child over twelve." By attaching the aesthetic value of the book to an age ceiling, specifically one commonly associated with puberty, Benig implies that other anthologies feature not real children but rather some less pure, teen-tainted mixture. This logic disqualifies even Benig's students from authorial status after turning twelve. He implicitly sets a deadline for his students' involvement in the publication process. The definite, intentionally limiting statements of the first three numbered points appear to justify the swaggering predictions of the future that follow: "it will make money." At the same time, however, Benig launches his students into the timeline of the editorial process with his discussion of Randy Cook. The fourth numbered point, on Cook—whose drawings Grove would ultimately decline to print— combines the future, present, and present perfect tenses in an assertion of one boy's temporal mobility: "the book *will be illustrated* by Randy Cook . . .

whose samplings *can be seen.* . . . Randy *has already won* a scholarship" (italics mine). The discussion of Cook works against the elegiac time-telling of child writers by portraying their ongoing collaboration as an exciting selling point of the anthology. Benig's drive for literary freshness alternately deploys and disrupts restrictive forms of time-telling about young authors.

This conflicting presentation of children's temporal relationship to publication culminates in the persuasively paradoxical claim "the book will have a political and social impact far out of proportion to its intent." Boasting modesty and intending unintentionality, the statement rests its twisted logic on the multiply agential nature of cross-age literary production. Texts derive meaning, he seems to imply, not from children's own writing acts but from their later reshaping and reception by adults. This cross-age doubling is reinforced by the word *proportion*, which contrasts the adult scale of "impact" with the appealing smallness of the under-twelve set. Benig's pitch highlights the divide between the timeline of children's writing and the timeline of the book-to-be as a literary selling point. But Benig's claim here can also be read with a wink. Flouting sequential logic, the statement ironically registers the temporal tangles that characterize youth anthologies, by which children are aged out of authorship, texts apparently accrue meaning only after the fact, and young writers anticipate these processes in their work. Benig's paradoxical promise of unintended success aligns these twists with the market pressures of the publishing industry, hinting at the engineering of surprise successes and the planning of novelty. His argument resonates with and may reflect the influence of his students' temporal tactics. His insistence on the power of the anthology to overtake its own time has already come to fruition in the overleaping, anticipatory texts of Yolanda Prescott and Deidre Harris.

After Grove was convinced to take on the project, Benig and his students found ways to disrupt the temporal order of publishing and bring children into the present of the editorial process. Throughout his communication with Grove, which began in April 1970, during the spring semester of his second school year with the class group, Benig constantly reminds the publisher that he is collaborating with the children even as he writes. He reports to Meeker, for instance, that "the children think each poem, etc. should be accompanied by a photograph of the author" in the book, which he begins to call "The Children (the title WE finally chose.)"[55] Benig's investment in real-time, cross-age collaboration included facilitating direct contact between Meeker and at least one child writer. Although Benig generally served as the liaison between the press and the children, young writer Mary Thomas sent one of her poems directly to Meeker, apparently at Benig's urging. Thomas's June 1970 missive serves to remind Grove that the children are continuing to produce book-worthy literature, even as both their time in Benig's classroom and the Grove manuscript process draw to a close. Although only Thomas's envelope, without the letter, remains in the archives, Meeker's extant reply to Thomas evidences the triangulation of communication among publisher, teacher-editor, and student writers.[56] The correspondence between Thomas and Meeker subtly scrambles the hierarchical protocol of the bookmaking process, according to which information and control flow from innocent child writers to enterprising teacher-collectors to powerful publishers, with a moment of multidirectional poetic conversation.

Meeker's response to Thomas concludes with a postscript: "PS When Mr. Benig called your piece 'the last word,' he meant 'it's the most,' or that he *really* liked it."[57] Meeker apparently finds Thomas to have misinterpreted Benig's colloquialism "the last word." Without Thomas's original note, it remains unclear whether she took the phrase to indicate the praiseworthy freshness of her poem, its potential placement at the end of the anthology, or a sense of closure or foreclosure within the publication process. Each of these possibilities raises questions of time and sequence in cross-age literary production. Although Meeker has "the last word" about "the last word" within the archive, taking on the typical adult role of assigning meaning to children's words, it is possible to imagine Thomas deploying the phrase in a way that reassigned meaning to Benig's original words and potentially commented on children's ability to intervene in the temporal politics of the publication process.

Benig and his students' revisions of authorial norms found limited purchase, even with a press as radical as Grove. For Benig, true collaboration involved not only bringing child writers into the editorial process but also including himself, like the children, as a source of textual raw material. Meeker rejected this cross-age integration when she refused Benig's petition that "[s]ince I too am a member of 5G-1, I would like to include two poems I've written (and which the kids like)."[58] Although Benig may have been a member of his classroom community, he was not one of "the children" and thus was expected to occupy a different role and stage of the bookmaking process. Indeed, the book title "WE finally chose," *The Children*, already barred Benig himself from that very plural first-person.

The conflicting visions of respective adult and child authorial roles in

The Children becomes visible in the confusion over author numbers. Benig initially pitched the book as the work of a class of "thirty-two children" as well as himself. By the final manuscript, he counted "19 girls/6 boys/1 man" as contributors, numbers consistent with the published anthology; six children presumably either did not produce writings deemed worthy of inclusion or did not provide permission for publication.[59] According to Benig's contract with Grove, each of the final twenty-six contributors would be paid equally for the book, whether adult editor or child poet, and whether contributing eight literary pieces or one. The contract stipulates: "The Author agrees to equally divide with the contributors all monies received.... In all cases, contributors' copies [of the book] are distributed by the author."[60] Accordingly, the permissions forms signed by the children's parents promise them a payment of $19.23—one twenty-sixth of the $500 advance—"as well as a percentage of any forthcoming royalties, which is to be divided equally among the 26 contributors."[61] Benig simultaneously stands as the sole *Author*, who receives all money and book copies first, and as one of many equal *contributors*, who await their compensation down the line.[62]

Perhaps confused by this attempt at equity, Grove staff mistakenly seized on this mixed-age total of twenty-six as the number of child contributors. The back cover of the book and its marketing materials declare that under the influence of Benig's teaching, "26 young students with reading difficulties, who hated school, who were frequently treated with hostility by teachers, found themselves in a class where their knowledge, curiosity, quickness of mind, and the daily terrors of their lives found expression."[63] The marketers' count here converts Benig, the twenty-sixth contributor, into a child in his own classroom. The number also equates classroom with anthology, disregarding the six noncontributing students that completed Benig's original count of thirty-two students. This flawed math parallels a disinterest in children's agential authorship. The blurb describes children as doubly "found," passive recipients of Benig's productive labor, rather than the generators of their own literary acts. The logic of time-telling narrates young people and their writings as the past-tense, fully explicable products of external factors.

The conflicting views of authorship at work in the publication process correspond to distinct timelines, as Benig's foreword to *The Children* reveals. In telling the story of his classroom, Benig variously uses *we* to group himself either with his students or with adult readers, whom his introduction clearly addresses. These first-person identities collide in the final lines of the foreword (italics mine): "Here are the children, the beautiful and always unpredictable children. Though *we* no longer see each other every morning, *we* will never really be apart./ Someday soon each of *us* will have to answer to *them* for what is being done to *them* and for what will be done to *them*. *They* will never forget."[64] In the very act of denying that he is *apart* from the children, Benig pivots from the *we* of his classroom to the *us* of the adult world, shunting the children from the first-person plural into the position of *them*. Articulating the children's future in double negatives—"will never really be apart," "will never forget"—Benig stretches his narrative between time-telling that freezes child writers in the past and a half-threatening, half-wistful promise of cross-age encounter "someday soon." His language enacts a clash characteristic of youth anthologies—between the timeline of child-adult literary collaboration and the timeline of adult-only, child-elegizing reception. At the same time, the conflating proximity of his first-person assignments presents the book as a potential space for the disruption of temporal order and the simultaneous presence of child writers and adult readers.

In the making of *The Children*, questions of authorship intertwine with claims about the last, the past, and the new. Benig's correspondence demonstrates how a white adult collaborator's fairly casual efforts to bring children into the real time of authorial control—while also securing a prestigious book contract—gradually slipped back into the stream of hierarchical, conventional order. Nevertheless, the playfully radical tone cultivated among Benig and his students left imprints in the archive that register young writers' active interrogation of the timelines of schooling and publication.

YOUNG WRITERS' EPHEMERA FOR POSTERITY

Benig's and his students' playful disruptions of the publication process, however limited in impact, were part of a larger product of epistolary experimentation with time and authorial control. A section of *The Children* called "Notes" features correspondence written by the children to Benig and to each other—mirroring the archival correspondence with Grove Press. Perhaps tellingly, I have found no mention of this section in critical reviews of *The Children*, suggesting the notes' confounding force. The notes intensify problems of agency and value already present in the interpretation of children's writings.

Passing notes in class, whether exchanging missives under desks during a math lesson or publicly distributing valentines, derives appeal not only from secrecy but from the channeling of otherwise directly spoken content into a different form, one with a particularly temporalized pleasure. When passing notes, the reader often observes the writer in the act of composition and waits to see the results of that furtive activity. The writer then watches and waits for reaction as the reader receives, opens, and absorbs the note, perhaps choosing to initiate a response and thus reverse the process. Even when writers slip messages into a desk or bag for later reading, notes are at least ostensibly ephemera, intended for a finite and relatively brief timeline. When published in the anthology, then, the notes attain an apparently undersigned afterlife, indulging voyeurism by later readers. Despite this performance of temporal innocence, the authors of *The Children* likely composed at least some of their notes with an eye to the immortal aspirations of other literary genres. The writers thus match the irony of Benig's claim to Grove that the "impact" of the book would exceed its "intent." The resulting ephemera for posterity open a space of inquiry into the ethics and politics of publishing children's writings.

The first entry in the "Notes" section, a letter to Benig by nine-year-old student Arnold Shuman, enacts a dance of revealing and withholding intimate information from his reader(s) that problematizes the act of telling.

> Dear Mr. Benig,
> I could not do my homework because something happened. I can't tell you what happened because if I do tell you don't tell nobody else. What happened is that my mother and my father had a fight. Then my mother said you get out of this house and my father have a saw in his hand and my mother had a knife in her hand and then my grandmother came and called the cops then they went fighting for Friday Saturday and Sunday.
>
> But I'm sorry that I
> couldn't do my homework
>
> from Arnold Shuman[65]

By explicitly disclosing what he states that he cannot, Shuman charges his note with transgressive intimacy. The letter becomes a small violation in the wake of larger violence, denoted by the repeated verb *happened*. The second sentence of the note encapsulates its ironic core, setting the terms for telling in the very act of explaining the impossibility of telling. By hinging this contradiction on the conjunction *because*, instead of *but*, Shuman suggests that, in a way, he sticks to his original promise of silence: he is not really telling but only writing a note about his homework, with details intended to reach "nobody else." The strain of syntax between past and present tenses suggests the tension of this arrangement. As Shuman "can't tell you," so he passes on that assignment of not-telling to his reader and teacher: "if I do tell you don't tell nobody else." As not-telling becomes a form of telling, so the apology for an uncompleted assignment comes to serve as substitute *homework*, a *work* of/from *home*.

While the obvious irony of Shuman's note is that Benig did tell somebody else, through the anthology publication, the implications of this apparent violation remain unclear. Like Mirthes's *Times* "Epilogue," *The Children* seems unconcerned with the potential repercussions of disclosure for young writers and their families. Printed without commentary in an ethnographically tinged publication package, Shuman's text assumes a default nonfiction status, but it may be fictional. If the children were as involved in the bookmaking process as Benig's correspondence with Grove claims, then Shuman likely agreed to the printing of his letter. Benig obtained a release form to print the work, neatly signed by "Mrs. Minnie Shuman," likely Arnold's mother or another family caretaker. Because the release forms listed texts by title alone, rather than attaching full copies of them—in this case, referring Shuman's note by the innocuous label, "Dear Mr. Benig, I could not do my homework"—Minnie Shuman may easily have never seen the text in question.[66] This obscurity of textual operation and circulation raises the question: if the printing of the text is riddled with irony, whose irony is it? Traditionally, irony is in the hands of the author, who controls what characters and audiences know at various times. To ask *who* and *when* of the irony of Shuman's note is to interrogate the nature of its authorship as published in *The Children*. These issues, moreover, have already been implied in Shuman's textual confrontation with disclosure. The published form of the letter thus represents a joint discussion by Benig and Shuman about the centrality of time and sequence to the meanings and consequences of classroom writing. In this way, student notes in *The Children* both generically and thematically come to resemble, and perhaps influence, the sometimes tussling correspondence between Benig and his editor Meeker.

The "Notes" section continues this confrontation with temporal power with texts written by students to each other. Kathy Lawson and Deborah Fulton's back-and-forth note tests and reestablishes the terms of their relationship through a negotiation of textual sequence.

Dear Deborah,
If you are not talking to me anymore and not my friend I am going to sit next to someone else for the rest of the year and play with someone else.

Write back and
write neat.
                    From Kathy Lawson

Dear Kathy,
If you're not talking to me or my friend I won't be yours.
Write back.

Dear Deborah,
Are you or not!?
Write back.

Dear Kathy,
Are you my friend? Yes or no.
Write back.

Dear Deborah,
If you are mine.
Write back.

O.K.[67]

Kathy and Deborah, both ten years old, pull each other back into official friendship through writing assignments to each other: "Write back and / write neat." The correspondents' mutual prompting playfully surrogates their teacher's role. They were likely alert to the irony that even as they explicitly assigned each other to write, their teacher was, overtly or implicitly, prompting them. Like most school assignments, the correspondents' directives to each other are invested in sequential order. In a kind of disarmament negotiation, Kathy and Deborah each craft their responses in an effort to make the other relent first in extending the hand of friendship. Deborah answers Kathy's initial "if" with another "if" threat and matches Kathy's question with another question. Kathy evades Deborah's demand for a "Yes or no" by returning to the realm of "if," but this time with a positive conditional: "If you are mine." This answer appears to satisfy Deborah, who can now abandon the formal apparatus of letter writing to jot merely, "O.K." The correspondents seem to have inched close enough for understanding without either sacrificing her dignity.

Kathy and Deborah likely voluntarily shared their exchange with Benig, though it is possible that he found, confiscated, or otherwise obtained some of the student-to-student notes in *The Children*. In the 1960s spirit of found poetry, experimental writing and nontraditional literacy pedagogy, Benig may have encouraged the passing of notes and made clear his interest in reading these texts. Though they resemble the surreptitious missives smuggled away from teachers' eyes in traditional classrooms, these student notes differ because they likely anticipate adult attention. Transformed into a kind of voluntary assignment—the "classwork" analogue to Arnold Shuman's "homework"—student notes become audience-conscious, cross-age performances, which both grant interpersonal access and examine its terms. Kathy and Deborah's note thus operates both on the timeline of ephemera, through their direct address to each other, and on the timeline of publication, by anticipating an implicit audience.

This double purpose of the note allows Kathy and Deborah's sequential contest to resonate with the process of cross-age literary production. Even as the correspondents cautiously reestablish their own intimacy, readers of the published book enjoy intimate access to this apparently private exchange. It is because the act of writing is a vulnerable one that Kathy and Deborah's mutual indulgence of requests to "write back" can rebuild the foundation of their friendship. Each cautiously avoids being the first, the one whose written words could be exploited by another. This sense of authorial risk parallels the classroom anthology genre, in which young writers rarely possess "the last word" on their own texts. Kathy and Deborah's prompts to "write back" thus suggest a double meaning, by which the children urge each other to *write/right back at them*, using authorship to disrupt race- and age-weighted structures of temporal control.

The notes of Benig's students and their published afterlives resonate with one of the handful of women's contributions to the Black Arts anthology *Black Fire*. Odaro's verse "Alafia" presents itself as a preface to her submission of poetry for the anthologists' consideration:

> I am writing at the request of
> Larry Neal, Ed Spriggs and Harold Foster
> Who seem to think that you
> Might be interested in my
> Poetry
> [. . . .]

> I am 20 years Black, born in
> Harlem
> Poverty's little girl
> Black Woman, Queen of the World [68]

Odaro's letter both succeeds and fails: none of the other pieces that it introduces were included in the anthology, suggesting that "Alafia" was included primarily for its epistolary charm. But by crafting a title, rhythm, rhyme, and line breaks, Odaro seems to have anticipated and leveraged that appeal. This charm, moreover, is inextricable from her aged and gendered identity as a sarcastically self-proclaimed "little girl." Odaro's "Alafia" demonstrates the affinity of young writers' epistolary entries with Black Arts innovations in literary form, particularly poets' experiments with the possibilities of replicating a sense of real-time, live encounter on the printed page.

THE TROUBLE WITH EPILOGUES

Classroom writers, as well as their adult collaborators, call attention to the centrality of narrative time within the processes that have bound children to racialized calendars of schooling, aged them out of authorship, and dictated the pathological foreclosure of their futures. Young writers expose time-telling—the threat of temporal domination in storytelling form—and craft alternative philosophies of temporality, sequence, and causality that reimagine the terms of American childhood and social order at large.

Classroom writers' temporal engagements demand attention to the storytelling work of this book. They provide me tools to watch for my own tendency to use the rubric of age to contain creative lives or to fall into an elegiac mode that performs writers' loss. Rachel Conrad's decision to omit ages in her discussions of young poets models this awareness; though I include writers' ages in order to shed light on their experiences and historical contexts, I agree with the spirit of Conrad's decision. [69] Academics know well the convenience of writing about those dead and gone, a trope into which Mirthes's *New York Times* "Epilogue," with its portrayal of bleached-blond Carmen's fall from child authorship, seems to fall. With important exceptions, such as Yolanda Prescott, I have not found most of the writers featured in this book, due to children's pen names, discarded press records, and other factors. By reading for children's own conceptions of time, I aim to acknowledge the continuation of young writers' creative lives beyond the years of classroom-bound adolescence.

Confronting the racial politics of time and age, child writers transform their transitory, temporally bounded status into a potent tool of critique, imagination, and self-inquiry. Classroom writers advance age-specific forms of the temporal tactics of anti-racist struggle. These young people invite a continuing, intergenerational conversation about the ways we use storytelling and narrative structures to understand marginalized children and their creative acts.

CHAPTER 3

Agency in Absentia

The Me Nobody Knows
Onstage

Dear Mr. Grady. . . . I've been thinking and writing a book on my life. I
wonder what would become of it, how many pages would I get?

Audiences at the 1970–71 hit musical *The Me Nobody Knows* heard the
young actor José Fernandez voice the words in this chapter's epigraph in
the character of Carlos.[1] Though Fernandez was a professional actor on a typical Broadway stage, the words he spoke had a more unusual status: they came
from an actual letter sent by C. R., an incarcerated teenaged boy, to a former
teacher. In language similar to a parent's query about the future of a child, C.
R. presciently muses about the potential of his literary work. Interspersed at
four points in the musical, Carlos's letters to Mr. Grady remind audiences to
approach the show as more than just another professional concoction like its
main rival that year, Stephen Sondheim's *Company*.[2] Unlike other Broadway
hits, *The Me Nobody Knows* was a staging of words written by children.

The Me Nobody Knows (known as *The Me*) is a musical adaptation of a
popular 1969 anthology, *The Me Nobody Knows: Children's Voices from the
Ghetto*, in which schoolteacher Stephen M. Joseph gathered his students'
writings with those collected by eleven other New York City teachers from
"most[ly] . . . Black or Puerto Rican" students, aged "seven to eighteen."[3]
The anthology captured the interest of Herb Schapiro, a white teacher and
aspiring playwright in New Jersey who sought to "brin[g] theater to places

where it was not much available . . . in prisons and in down-and-out urban settings." After experimental performances of the anthology—including making "a short nonmusical film . . . in Trenton's streets," with anthology texts performed "by local residents"—Schapiro collaborated with lyricist Will Holt and composer Gary William Friedman to create a full musical.[4] The result reversed Schapiro's interest in importing theater to underserved venues by instead bringing the words of marginalized young people into the mainstream theater world. Schapiro and his partners wove together approximately eighty children's poetry and prose writings from the anthology into spoken and sung roles for six boys and six girls. The authorial note in the show program and libretto, crediting all spoken lines to the child anthology contributors and the lyrics for all but four of the musical numbers to adults, hints at the complexities of textual preserving, splicing, melding, and reshaping in *The Me*'s speeches and songs.[5]

Moving and dancing around a spare, multilevel set, the characters of *The Me* loosely relate to each other through a minimal plotline. Their collage of voices expresses friendship and teasing, love and lust, boredom with school, existential musings, and frustration with the drugs, violence, racism, and poverty of New York life. Having caught the attention of influential critics while off-Broadway, the musical soon began its award-winning run at the Helen Hayes and Longacre Theatres on Broadway before appearing in several other cities and countries. With a live TV version running on *Showtime* in 1980, *The Me* is still produced in schools and local theaters today.

The glittering mobility of the show contrasts with the circumstances of C. R. and many of the other young authors whose words graced the stage. The contributors to *The Me Nobody Knows* were minimally involved, if at all, with the production of the anthology and even less included in its adaptation into a musical. In fact, some of the young authors behind the musical may have never learned of its existence, even as the show spread around the country and the world. Jerry Parker's 1971 *Newsday* piece "Gathering the 'Me' Almost Nobody Knew" turns this unusual situation into a publicity gimmick. "By the time a hit show has passed its 280th performance, has a second company on the boards in Chicago and others set to open in Munich and London, it's high time the authors had a look at it," Parker reports. "Unfortunately, only 34 of the 80 writing talents could be rounded up to attend the special authors' night" performance of *The Me* at the Helen Hayes Theatre.[6]

Where were the forty-six missing writers whose absence haunted Parker's jaunty tone? Anthology editor Joseph told Parker: "'Some are in Vietnam, some are in reform school, some are at Princeton'. . . . At least one of the authors, Joseph added, has died—of an overdose of heroin.'"[7] Joseph's point- edly incomplete report alludes to the conditions of constraint imposed on Black and Puerto Rican children in circa-1970 New York. In contrast to the civil rights dream of young people's desegregation, mobilization, and mingling, the reentrenchment and renormalization of de facto segregation in schools and neighborhoods, along with an increasingly racial discrepancy in unemployment, curtailed the movement of young bodies. Young people's basic mobility, meanwhile, was increasingly foreclosed throughout the late 1960s and early 1970s ramp-up of the War on Crime. As Elizabeth Hinton has demonstrated, the "War on Poverty" declared by President Lyndon Johnson in 1964 went hand in hand with a "War on Crime," rooted in the increasingly ambitious, sophisticated, and well-funded surveillance and con- trol of the very people that the War on Poverty purported to save. Both overt policing and surveillance-laced social service programs centrally targeted the young, which cultivated a self-perpetuating cycle of scrutiny, crime statistics, and interventions and ultimately created an environment that criminalized "such everyday activity as getting a late-night snack in segregated urban neighborhoods."[8] Even as these systems worked to keep young bodies in place, coercive journeys to carceral institutions and Vietnam turned travel into another form of entrapment. C. R. and the other young authors of *The Me* were victims of, witnesses to, and commentators on fundamental devel- opments in the post–civil rights American racial order, including the buildup toward what would ultimately be recognized as mass incarceration.

The Me writers' inability to access the staging of their work thus resulted from the same conditions of age, race, and class marginalization central to the appeal of the anthology and musical. A key *The Me* writer makes this contrast clear in a separate 1972 newspaper interview. Emphasizing the luck involved in his own path to college at Brandeis, Lloyd Corbin (pen name: Djangatolum) demands: "'I mean, man, how does it figure? I lived on a block with 200 to 300 kids and only two of us, two! of! us!, were able to get out, to get a chance at college. But what about the rest of them in there, who's gonna help?'"[9] Corbin's emphasis on the space of the block marks the racist geography faced by young people of his generation. *The Me* promised largely white, affluent audiences intimate access to minoritized children even while maintaining those children's remoteness from Broadway.

These dynamics of absence and presence pervaded 1960s–1970s youth writing beyond the exceptional case of *The Me*'s Broadway run. Particularly in the loose legal landscape of authorial rights before the 1976 Copyright Act, children's writings moved fluidly among adult hands and venues, but the writers were often granted little recognition, control, or profit themselves. This casual circulation is illustrated in the reminiscence of C. R.'s teacher and correspondent, Mr. Grady. Ed Grady later recalled supplying texts for *The Me Nobody Knows* anthology: "When Steve Joseph asked me for some writings my students had done while I was teaching at the Youth House . . . I gave him a brown envelope stuffed with things they had written, letters to me, a movie script, et al. . . . Some time later Steve returned my envelope and told me the book would be out soon."[10] Though this account, written decades after the fact, may reflect Grady's imperfect recollection of the anthologization process, the adult-to-adult handoff of the "brown envelope" suggests how easily young people could be excluded from the journeys of their own writings. Putting Grady's account next to that of Corbin, moreover, reveals how public attention to youth voices operated in close relation with the public neglect and policing of young people. The intimacy of youth circulation and incarceration, youth influence and disempowerment, takes dramatic form in the story of *The Me* musical.

If young writers' absence proved suspiciously convenient to the showmakers, it also heightened a theme prevalent in the children's work. Even while reinforcing the constraints on young writers of color, the musical also showcased their literary contestations of those limits. *The Me* authors theorize the risky but powerful process of creating within adult and/or white structures of power. In an era in which government agencies worked literally to take Black and Latinx boys "out of circulation," in the chilling words of a Los Angeles police captain, young writers use adult interest to put their writings *into* circulation.[11] Living with incomplete independence of movement and voice, young people dispatch their words where they cannot bodily go—as if predicting the dramatic journeys of their work away from their own lives. *The Me* writers generate forms of what I term *agency in absentia*, forms of creative influence exerted at a distance. These forms both mark and exceed the limits imposed on young writers by age, race, class, and gender.

Through their figurations of absence, *The Me* authors provide tools for addressing the distance of children from the textual record that has long haunted studies of childhood and childhood literature. Karen Sanchéz-Eppler notes a persistent academic "insistence on the lost, hollow, absent status of the child, who can only ever enter this scholarly field as a product of adult imagining, something we adults project and shape with our desire and our study." To combat this convention, Marah Gubar usefully proposes a "kinship model of childhood," emphasizing the closeness and similarity between children and adults in order to surface actual young people's role in children's literature.[12] I argue that even as scholars increasingly work against the hollow-child model and toward children's literary presence, absence remains analytically useful, deepening our understanding of the ways in which marginalized young people have left their mark and interpreted their own circumstances.

The affinity of childhood and performance makes the theater especially rich ground for examining young writers' interpretations of childhood absence. Robin Bernstein argues that childhood itself is a form of performance driven by loss, as growth imposes a continual disappearing act on the state of childhood. This loss-driven quality of childhood, Bernstein demonstrates, has historically been recruited in support of American racism—a phenomenon to which 1960s–1970s youth writers repeatedly call our attention.[13] Drawing on Black studies theories of fugitivity, the concept of agency in absentia illuminates the ways in which young people themselves, as well as adults, have imaginatively deployed the figure of the missing child as a tool for interrogating and reimagining their lives and social worlds.[14] In *The Me*, young writers explore a trope of haunting absence that both contests essentializing discourses of authenticity and visibility and reckons with the terror of young people's real disappearances by violence and incarceration.

In the off-Broadway and Broadway productions of *The Me*, children's development of disembodied agency via written words was accentuated by their reembodiment in the performances of professional actors. The resulting play of absence and presence generated a drama of its own, staging the contrast between the mobility of children's written words and the unfreedom of children's embodied lives. Animated with this drama of youth writing, *The Me* reveals the relevance of childhood to key debates in theater and performance during and after the civil rights movement. In the 1960s, theater makers increasingly sought to apply the principles of civil rights to the stage with tactics ranging from cross-racial casting—such as the representation of Shakespearean characters by non-white actors—to the founding of community-based, minority-controlled theaters. These developments raised challenging questions for theatermakers and theatergoers alike: How should actors' bodies be interpreted? How does racial identity affect acting and its reception? What are right and wrong ways of interpreting and staging a script, and what does it mean to stay true to a playwright's vision?[15] *The Me* brought children's own words and lives to bear on these questions, which continue to charge theatrical productions today. As *The Me*'s adult showmakers remapped eighty child poets onto twelve dramatic roles, then played by young performers selected for stage appeal, the stories of marginalized neighborhoods lit up the affluent city center, and children's voices filled adult-dominated spaces of consumption. The adaptation process depended on erasure of the texts' origins, leaving the musical with an unsettling palimpsestic quality. Issues of casting, authorship, and agency were heightened by the complexity of the relationship of page and stage, or what Ju Yon Kim identifies as the loaded space of racial discourse "between paper and performance." In *The Me*, as in the theatrical work analyzed by Kim, the simultaneously close and dissonant relationship between a theatrical production and the written texts on which it is based holds racial meanings beyond the overt content onstage.[16]

This chapter examines agency in absentia in work by three contributors to *The Me*, all of whom seem to be gendered male. This focus on boy writers heeds Michael J. Dumas and Joseph Derrick Nelson's call for forms of Black boyhood studies that contest discourses of Black male crisis by "privileg[ing] how Black boys imagine and express their own senses of self." Following Simone C. Drake's urging to seek Black boys' own creative perspectives in culture, I approach literature and performance as spaces where Black and Puerto Rican boys have worked within and beyond their positioning in narratives of crisis.[17]

As C. R. turns to letters to recruit support where he cannot bodily go, two other teenaged boy authors, Akmir-U-Akbar and Curtis M., use short fiction to develop the respective concepts of powerful haunting and advantageous obscurity. These writers collectively showcase a trope of paradoxically powerful absence and self-consciously emphasize their own authorship through metaliterary writing about writing. With these tactics, C. R., Akmir-U-Akbar, and Curtis M. both express and surpass the particular conditions of danger and unfreedom imposed on Black and Latinx boys in the era of the War on Crime. Looking ahead to the disembodied travels of their texts, writers both implicitly and explicitly, in the words of C. R., "wonder what would become of" their texts.

Here, as in the preceding chapters, I embrace the apparent interpretative fallacy of reading for young writers' anticipation and prescience. Anticipation may name what has, as of yet, been deferred from the dominant cultural stage, as modeled by Nina Simone in her ironic aside to her 1964 Carnegie Hall performance of "Mississippi Goddam": "This is a show tune but the show hasn't been written for it yet."[18] Anticipating the journeys of their texts across age and other structures of power, circa-1970 children participate in a radical anti-racist practice of encountering the future as a site of both injustice and liberation.

AGENCY BY MAIL: C. R.'S EPISTOLARY ACTS

The twisting travels of the letters to Mr. Grady demonstrate young writers' distancing from their texts. C. R., a seventeen-year-old resident of an upstate "state training school," wrote the letters to Grady, a white teacher from C. R.'s time in New York's notoriously abusive Spofford Youth House.[19] After the letters' publication in *The Me Nobody Knows* anthology, the musical creators obtained licensing rights from the anthology publishers to use the letters and changed their signature from "Sincerely, C. R." to "Sincerely, Carlos." As a first draft of the script for *The Me* indicates (fig. 4), the theatrical adapters literally collaged pieces of anthology text, which were cut out of the book and pasted onto script pages. The adapters then went through with a pink pen to trim words and sentences from the children's texts and assign the words to distinct roles, adding typewritten stage notes and song lyrics. For instance, one child's prose piece was divided into a conversation among several characters. In this early draft, C. R.'s voice appears in two long speeches, assigned in a pink jotting to "José [Fernandez, the actor]"; ultimately, all four of C. R.'s letters, abridged and rearranged, would enter the script.[20] While the visible traces of manual copy-pasting and penning in the drafted script clearly show adult selection, revision, and organization, similar acts likely shaped the written anthology as well. The apparently original texts spliced into dramatic form were themselves products of adult adaptation. C. R. himself may or may not have learned about the long itinerary of his letters, particularly while incarcerated. But given his attention to the possibilities of literary influence, he may not have been completely surprised.

Scripted to Carlos in four epistolary interludes throughout the musical, C. R.'s letters theatricalize the acts of writing from which the show originated.[21] As the element closest to ongoing plot in the musical, as well as a particularly explicit moment of cross-genre adaptation, the letters exert special influence

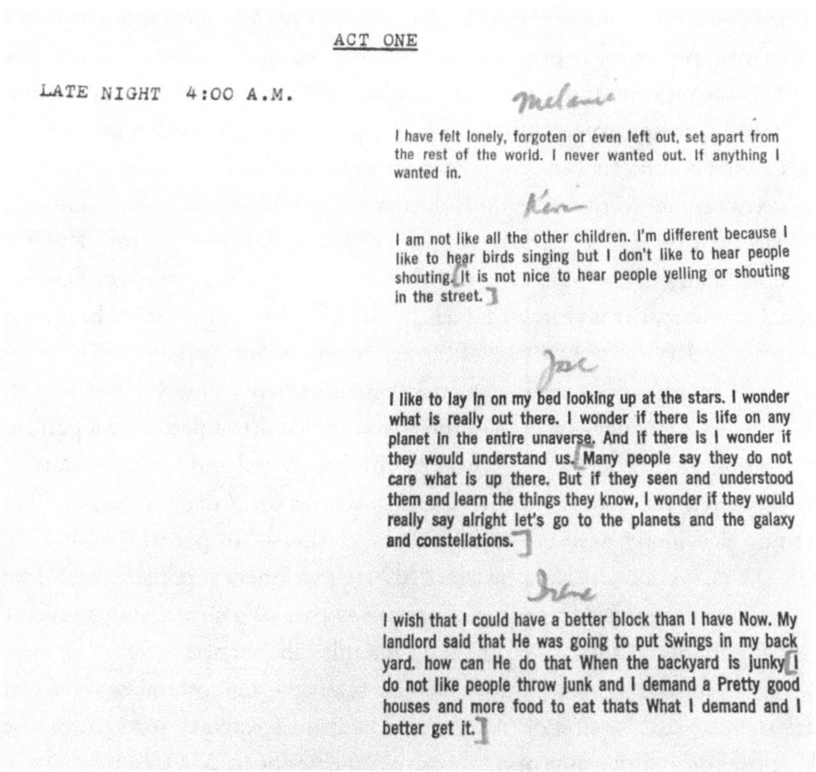

ACT ONE

LATE NIGHT 4:OO A.M.

melanie

I have felt lonely, forgotten or even left out, set apart from the rest of the world. I never wanted out. If anything I wanted in.

Kevin

I am not like all the other children. I'm different because I like to hear birds singing but I don't like to hear people shouting. It is not nice to hear people yelling or shouting in the street.

Joe

I like to lay in on my bed looking up at the stars. I wonder what is really out there. I wonder if there is life on any planet in the entire universe. And if there is I wonder if they would understand us. Many people say they do not care what is up there. But if they seen and understood them and learn the things they know, I wonder if they would really say alright let's go to the planets and the galaxy and constellations.

Irene

I wish that I could have a better block than I have Now. My landlord said that He was going to put Swings in my back yard. how can He do that When the backyard is junky I do not like people throw junk and I demand a Pretty good houses and more food to eat thats What I demand and I better get it.

FIGURE 4. Page from the "First Draft" libretto of *The Me Nobody Knows* musical. Gift of Will Holt, 1970, Billy Rose Theatre Division, New York Public Library. —Courtesy of the estate of Will Holt.

over the audience's interpretation of the musical. They also stand out formally in the show, evoking the increasingly popular subgenre of epistolary theater.[22] Leveraging this stylistic force, Carlos's epistolary voicing highlights C. R.'s ability to dispatch his literary influence where he himself cannot bodily go.

C. R. achieves this agential extension through the rhetorical cultivation of his second-person patron(s): Grady directly and, by extension, the mostly white, privileged audiences of Broadway. C. R./Carlos makes that surrogacy particularly inviting by emphasizing his intimacy with and gratitude for his addressee. "You're like a father to me. Mr. Grady, all the things you have done for me, I don't know how to thank you," the writer tells his absent correspondent. "You're the only one I can really express my feelings to. . . . What would

I do without you Mr. Grady? Whom could I write to, when I write or think about you, my mind is put to ease."[23] By becoming that person who hears Carlos's feelings in an uncaring world, the audience of *The Me* can assume the second-person role of the heroic listener, whose very reception of Carlos's words becomes a beneficent act at the moment of his own community's apparent failure. At the same time, the explicit privacy of the correspondence throws light on the voyeuristic edge of the musical. Like the title, "The Me Nobody Knows," Carlos's praise for Mr. Grady generates a paradox of exceptional intimacy, through which each holder of a Broadway ticket becomes, together and alone, "the only one I can really express my feelings to."

I refer to audience members as ticket-holders here to mark the extent to which C. R.'s language resembles the transactional art of flattering a patron. The writer credits Mr. Grady with not only emotional and readerly support but also material provision. Interspersing thanks for a diary and "smooth"-writing pen along with requests for new clothes—"In pants I wear 32 × 32"—C. R. literally dresses himself in his correspondent's sponsorship.[24] His repetitions of grateful dependence appear as part of a strategic dynamic of exchange between a young writer and his adult collaborator.

Apparent in the musical, this give-and-take appears even more vividly in the anthologized version of the letters. The third epistolary segment in *The Me* closes on a fairly conventional note of indebtedness: "Mr. Grady you have brought happiness into my life. How can I do the same for you? Sincerely, Carlos." The anthologized version, in contrast, transitions directly from a discussion of gifts: "I like royal blue for a color [of shirt]. So Mr. Grady, you've bought happyness into my life, how can I do the same for you? Just give me your wish and it will be granted." By shifting C. R.'s *bought* to Carlos's *brought*, the musical downplays the writer's sly acknowledgement of the "royal" intertwining of material and emotional backing. The genie-like invitation to "give me your wish" is more than rhetorical. C. R. claims not only the desire but also the capacity to pay back his adult patron, such as by sending "a few pictures of the things we do [at reform school] and how the place looks." In a canny reading of the cultural market, C. R. knew his ability to provide content on marginalized youth and to fulfill adult desires through the emotional labor of correspondence. The latter possibility finds support in the closing line of the anthologized letter: "So please excuse this letter for being so short and all mistakes I may have made in it."[25] Especially given that the letter is, in fact, fairly long, this final sentence appears as the flourish of a self-conscious writer performing epistolary etiquette to his patron. The apology ironically calls attention to the skills of the writer and the status of the letter as a gift, reinforcing C. R.'s constant rhetorical work to establish a dynamic of mutual gratitude and exchange between himself and his adult patron. In light of this labor, C. R. can be read as delivering a final set of gifts in anticipation of future audiences: his anthology publication and his contribution to the musical itself. If the adult scripters of *The Me* attempt to downplay his playfully favor-currying side to lean toward the sentimental, that adjustment demonstrates the resilient capacity of C. R.'s writing to adjust to a new set of patrons and their "wish[es]," even in the absence of the writer himself.

C. R.'s reference to the quality and length of his missive typifies a self-conscious fascination with his own writing that recurs throughout his letters, including their scripting for stage. When first requesting that Mr. Grady send a blank notebook, C. R./Carlos muses, "I'd like to have a diary, in this way, I can keep a record of myself, and little things I say and do."[26] He reports constantly on the use of that diary and his sense of himself as a writer. In fact, he not only "keep[s] a record of himself" but also begins to document his incoming and outgoing correspondence, a metaliterary act worthy of a writer who anticipates his own archiving. While the letters to Mr. Grady maintain an intimate tone, they also cast an eye outward, as if anticipating their own publicity far beyond a student-teacher exchange.

The central conflict of the letters fittingly focuses on writing itself. Since arriving upstate, C. R. laments, he has received no letters from family or friends, other than Mr. Grady. The messages to his former teacher, then, may function partly as a means for C. R. to gather literary support and skill and to rehearse the epistolary art of repairing relationships. His repeated testaments to the emotional effects of Mr. Grady's own letters, a sweetness that C. R. contrasts to the pain of his family's silence—"Just to know someone cared made me feel like a real person"—also serve as observations of the emotional and persuasive powers that letter writing can unleash. In the last letter in both the anthology and the musical, the narrative arc concludes with a writing triumph: the letters home have finally elicited responses. As he reports to Mr. Grady: "I did just what you told me to. I wrote everybody in my family and I just knew that I would hear from someone. My sister wrote me and my girl friend came back to me. So I'm the happyest boy or man in the world today."[27] C. R. celebrates not only his reconciliation with loved ones but also the power of his "smooth"-writing pen: he has used his words to call on and renew his relationships with others. He associates that success, moreover, with his own coming of age, identifying himself as teetering on the line between "boy" and "man." The context of C. R.'s authorial self-awareness suggests a nuanced reading of his statement to Mr. Grady that "I did just what you told me to." While Mr. Grady may have provided the teacherly prompt, C. R. himself has done the writing, as both correspondents know well. The statement of obedience maintains the etiquette of crediting a patron while also ironically marking the limits of patronage and gesturing toward the writer's sense of his own power.

In their very success, C. R.'s letters mark the distance between his own constraints as an incarcerated minor and the mobility of his written work. In this way, C. R. prepares his texts to join the genre of the imprisoned author's open letter, emblematized by the 1963 "Letter from a Birmingham Jail" of Martin Luther King, Jr. Likely writing close to the time that Etheridge Knight published his 1968 volume *Poems from Prison*, C. R. can be seen as participating in the Prison Arts Movement, which, as Lee Bernstein notes, joined the Black Arts, Black Power, and Puerto Rican Movements in addressing conditions found both within and outside prison walls: "limited control, consistent physical and ideological oppression, and the daily experience of racism." Writer Piri Thomas recalls of his incarceration as a young adult in the 1950s: "'They only got my body, not my mind.' I promised myself not to serve time, but rather make time serve me. . . . I learned to transpose [my] feelings into words."[28] C. R. contributes to this theorization of artmaking under bodily constraint, demonstrating incarcerated minors' participation in the development of prison arts. His happy ending, in all its incompleteness, results from his artful delegation of agency to the page, which can travel far beyond him—to Mr. Grady, into his family members' hearts, through the scripted character of Carlos, onto José Fernandez's stage, and into this chapter.

THE PEN THAT GUIDES THE HAND: AKMIR-U-AKBAR'S GHOSTLY WRITER

Eighteen-year-old Akmir-U-Akbar, formerly Leroy Carter, uses science fiction to anticipate the divergence of young authors' personal and textual fates. Recited by the character Clorox immediately after the first letter to Mr. Grady, U-Akbar's parable, "The Transformation," shares with C. R.'s letters a self-conscious exploration of authorial possibilities and limits in absentia.

U-Akbar's tale provides a metaphor for young writers' ability to turn painful absence into rhetorical power.[29]

"The Transformation" begins: "Problems arise when one must strain to produce new inventions in my type of work. Recently I was taken by surprise when a pile of synthetic type material fell upon me. Desperately trying to escape I found myself transformed into a pen."[30] U-Akbar's story may have influenced the *Boston Globe* critic who praised the "Kafkaesque" nightmares of the *Me Nobody Knows* anthology.[31] Similar to Gregor of Kafka's *Metamorphosis*, U-Akbar's narrator transforms under pressure, literal and figurative, at work in a "plastic corporation."[32] The unnamed protagonist's new identity as a pen associates him with yet another form of labor, that of the minority youth writer himself. With few and shrinking opportunities for literal manufacturing jobs, poor city neighborhoods in the 1960s partly operated instead as factories of cultural and ethnographic material, run by War on Poverty programs and what Robin Kelley sardonically deems "the new ethnographic army."[33] U-Akbar slyly comments on this "strain to produce" imposed on young writers of color by the American market packaging their texts for profit. Literalizing the traditional metonymy of the pen as a stand-in for the author, as in "the pen is mightier than the sword," he presents his pen-hero's industrial processing as a metaphor for the commodification of child writers. In fact, the fictional text of "The Transformation" itself could be the very kind of "new invention" that shapes the pen-hero's doom.

U-Akbar's story merges the science fiction thrill of experiments gone wrong with the working-class everyday of commodity production and consumption. After his remarkable change, the pen-hero is routed automatically onto the factory belt like any other pen. "Arriving at the assembly line I could feel a slight twitch in the refill of myself. I was being filled with ink." The uncanny feeling of being a thing, powerless yet lucid, clashes with the conforming force of the factory, which functions to produce unremarkable, unoriginal tools, as well as reliably unoriginal workers. That very process of mass production delivers the pen-hero to his redemption: "To my surprise I was shipped and put onto display in my community and bought by my younger brother. Fortunately he took care of things that he had to buy on his own. And as long as I still can hold onto my reserved refill, my brother's hand shall be guided by me."[34] With his pointed choice of the word "community," a central bureaucratic term of the War on Poverty, U-Akbar narrates the connection between labor and cultural exploitation and the extractive profiteering of consumer sales in poor neighborhoods of color, an issue brought to the fore by the targeting of stores during 1960s civil disorders. U-Akbar suggests that community and commodity become as inextricable as body and pen. It is within these seemingly intractable conditions that the pen-hero locates his power.

Helplessly metamorphosized by his imaginative work of invention, the pen-hero nevertheless possesses a certain, rather phallic potency, his refill barrel of ink. U-Akbar uses the surprising agency of an inanimate object to imagine a secret and unacknowledged artistic legacy. The concluding shift from past to present and future tense—"And as long as I still can hold onto my reserved refill, my brother's hand shall be guided by me"—suggests that, in a metaliterary twist, the pen itself may be writing this very story. As the "reserved refill" projects into the future, the pen-hero asserts his power to hold back information yet undisclosed and stories untold. At the same time, the pen-hero's conditional triumph hits its own sinister note with the question of just how he guides his younger brother's hand. Does the pen facilitate or manipulate his brother's authorial power? If the pen is mightier than the sword, is the hand still mightier than the pen, or does the pen resemble the tail that wags the dog? U-Akbar's tale of ghostly authorship positions these questions of children's literary agency and labor within the transformative landscape of US capitalism and inequality.

As a member of What's Happening, an influential extracurricular youth writing group in New York that produced a youth magazine of the same name, U-Akbar participated in a circle of young people savvy to mainstream America's interest in their voices. According to the group's adult adviser, Elaine Avidon, the *What's Happening* magazine had over one thousand subscribers and received fan mail from Langston Hughes and Muriel Rukeyser. Avidon remembers U-Akbar as an occasional visitor to the group and a memorable contributor to the magazine. Stephen M. Joseph, like many New York students and teachers, likely read the magazine and requested permission to reprint several texts from it in *The Me Nobody Knows*. Despite the emphatically youth-directed nature of What's Happening, however, U-Akbar likely did not have the opportunity to weigh in on his publication.[35]

Joseph prefaces U-Akbar's two pieces in the anthology by stating that the young writer died on October 17, 1967, not long after writing "The Transformation" and a year and a half before the release of *The Me Nobody Knows*.[36] While lending a poignant prescience to his posthumously published tale of loss and legacy, his death also makes vivid the limits of minority youth writers' authorial recognition and control. By tactically delegating agency to his text, U-Akbar anticipatorily "reserved [a] refill" for thinking through the disparate fates of children of color and their texts. As the pen-hero guides a hand with ghostly force, so the narrative structures a way of reading the power of young writers beyond their own embodied lives.

U-Akbar joins the postwar bending of science thrills into anti-racist forms. As a disturbing, even violent transformation of the body, the pen-hero's saga resonates with growing African American attention to medical racism, even before the horrific revelations of the Tuskegee Syphilis Experiment. Black artists both recruited science fiction into Afrofuturist visions and examined the dangers of scientific experimentation. Amiri Baraka's 1966 play *A Black Mass*, for instance, adapts the Nation of Islam founding story of Yakub, the misguided scientist who first created white people. More than a cautionary tale, Yakub allows Baraka, as Alondra Nelson has observed, to "allud[e] to (and revers[e]) the centuries-old processes through which medical and scientific practice have scrutinized, codified, classified, and otherwise constructed black bodies."[37] U-Akbar engages complexly with this discourse by making his pen-hero both the experimenter and the experimented-on.

The staging of "The Transformation" within *The Me* musical uncannily heightens U-Akbar's theme of simultaneous agency and manipulability. Clorox, originally played by Northern Calloway, delivers the pen-hero's story as an uninterrupted monologue. The character's name is drawn from another real contributor to the anthology, What's Happening member Frank Cleveland, who used the pen-name Clorox and authored two of the longest and most important speeches in the musical. The musical adapters folded into Clorox's voice several other teenaged male authors from What's Happening, including U-Akbar, who likely knew and worked closely with the real Clorox/Cleveland. Although U-Akbar's text is preserved untouched, at least from its anthologized version, the adult authors of the script instituted one major change: the character Clorox introduces the story as "THE TRANSFORMATION, by Clorox Johnson."[38] Whereas the reassignment of a text to another voice occurs throughout the musical, the explicit use of a byline is unique in the show. The adult adapters, then, went out of their way to emphasize Clorox as the author of U-Akbar's story.

The result paradoxically deepens the significance of U-Akbar's death by reinforcing his own theme of disembodied authorship. If live theater, as

Herbert Blau and other theorists have proposed, is charged by the possibility of an actor dropping dead at any time during the performance, *The Me* might also be animated by the potential of another writer losing his or her life—or more likely, aging out of his or her childhood life—while the Broadway show goes on, cast, crew, and audience unknowing.[39] U-Akbar has become a posthumous ghostwriter, with both the helplessness and haunting force that the term entails. His anonymity protects and even enhances his authorial influence. The erasure of U-Akbar's byline strengthens his alignment not only with his own nameless pen-hero but also with the unnamed Invisible Man of Ralph Ellison's 1952 novel. In his very distinction—"Nor is my invisibility exactly a matter of a biochemical accident to my epidermis"—Ellison's narrator relates his state to the transformations of science fiction. Powerfully unseen, the ghostly pen-hero and his posthumously renamed author echo the Invisible Man's "frighten[ed]" and frightening closing line: "Who knows but that, on the lower frequencies, I speak for you?"[40]

Moving from the "lower frequencies" of inanimate form, "The Transformation" positions the uplifting Broadway theater in the depths of the drama of youth writing. With metaliterary attention to his own authorship and figures of absence and haunting, U-Akbar set the stage both to interrogate the politics of authorship in *The Me* and to use the show as his own "reserved refill" of literary influence. The musical comes to express young people's absently agential writing acts, which both register and transcend the bodily realities faced by children of U-Akbar's generation.

THE TREE NOBODY KNOWS:
CURTIS M.'S CHALLENGE TO VISIBILITY

Akmir-U-Akbar's theme of invisibility extends into arguably the most visible text in *The Me* musical. Curtis M.'s short story was the only child-authored work provided on paper to theater audiences. "The Hopeless Tree" was printed as an epigraph in the show program, as well as in the libretto consulted by cast and crew. The text appeared unedited and unabridged from its anthology printing, except that while the anthology listed the author as "Curtis M.," the program credited "C. M.," perhaps to tighten alignment with the onstage character of Carlos. José Fernandez as Carlos first sang "The Tree," a musical adaptation of Curtis M.'s story in the second act of *The Me*. A quick glance down at the playbill amid the dim theater seats would have confirmed for audience members that the song lyrics slightly differed from the printed words and were credited to an adult creator of the show, Will Holt. The double provision of the story as both epigraph and song provided theatergoers with a glimpse into the musical makers' process of adapting the anthology texts, the transition from the byline of C. M. to the authorial crediting of Will Holt.

Even while operating as a tool of transparency, the story itself communicates suspicion of the clear and visible. Through a symbolic play of exposure and obscurity, Curtis M. anticipates his own doubled role in the spotlight and the shadows of Broadway, casting doubt on the premise of visibility politics and opening imaginative space for the mysteries of young life.

The Hopeless Tree

There was a man waiting under a baby apple tree. He was waiting for an apple to grow on it. He would just sit there and wait and wait but it never grew. He watered it every day but it just didn't grow. No matter what he did, it did not grow. So the man got discouraged and gave up hope for the tree. He wanted to cut it down. So one day he decided to do it. He said he would do it on a Sunday afternoon, rain or snow. So on Sunday there was a fog and he could not see the tree and so he did not cut it down.

The following Sunday a baby apple was hanging on it.

—C. M. [Curtis M.], age fourteen[41]

Curtis M.'s implicit moral of keeping patience with small, vulnerable growing things may allegorize adults' treatment of young people. The charming phrase "baby apple," with its gentle plosives and wide-mouthed vowels, resonantly suggests human children or perhaps their artistic creations, such as the story at hand. Curtis cultivates a sense of waiting and ritual delay, moving from Sunday to Sunday. The narrator's repeated use of "so," suggesting oral storytelling, signals the discrete and ordered stages of the tale, each in its own time, perhaps advancing a lesson about delicate timing and patience in the process of literary production particularly appropriate to a text that would be circulated and adapted over several years.

Beginning with its title, "The Hopeless Tree" resembles *The Giving Tree*, Shel Silverstein's 1964 picture book about a tree that gives shade, apples, branches, and eventually her trunk to the self-absorbed boy she loves, until nothing is left but a "tired" old man sitting on a stump.[42] Curtis's victimized apple tree, exploitative human, and matter-of-fact narrative tone could reflect the influence of Silverstein's popular and painful work. If Curtis follows *The Giving Tree*, however, he also reverses it, so that an adult impatiently awaits profit from a maturing tree, rather than the tree witnessing the growth and growing greed of the man. In Curtis's version, it is the younger figure who is, in Akmir-U-Akbar's language, under "strain to produce."

Curtis M.'s story also references a more universal required reading of the era. While Curtis and his peers may certainly have procured *The Giving Tree*, these young people likely knew all too well the kind of Founding Father worship that passed for reading material in many underfunded classrooms, whose textbooks bore titles such as *Heroes, Heroines, and Holidays* and *Great Names in American History*.[43] Curtis M. draws on this education in adulation to signify on a long-time staple of American classrooms, the legend of George Washington and the cherry tree. In this ubiquitous tale, young George frankly confesses to hacking up his father's beloved cherry tree with a new ax and is rewarded handsomely for his honesty: "I can't tell a lie."[44] Assata Shakur surfaces the irony of this lesson in her recollection of a school play from her childhood in late 1950s New York City: "I was cast as one of the cherry trees. . . . To sway from side to side and sing: 'George Washington never told a lie, never told a lie, he never told a lie. George Washington never told a lie, and the truth goes marching on'. . . . Here they had this old craka slavemaster, who didn't give a damn about Black people, and they had me, an unwitting little Black child, doing a play in his honor."[45] Shakur calls up her history as an adult-scripted child actor, required to perform as the very object of Washington's rewarded violence, to highlight the dishonest roots of an American founding fiction.

Disrupting the Washingtonian virtue of transparency, Curtis's fable hinges on obscurity. A veiling fog, an inability to see, prevents the man from felling the apple tree and allows the baby apple to emerge in its own time. "The Hopeless Tree" thus unsettles the easy valorization of bringing marginalized stories to light and making minority voices heard. Curtis's fog prompts attention to scrutinized and spotlighted minority youth authors' deployments of productive obscurity.

The musical staging of Curtis's work teeters between celebration and suspicion of transparency. Lyricist Will Holt's song version, "The Tree," immediately follows a monologue by the character Clorox.[46] Voicing the words of young author Tim Engel, Clorox recounts his horror at witnessing policemen's callous treatment of a distraught and injured Black man, who moans, as if prophesying the fate of his community, "They trahd to kill me, they trahing ta kill me . . ."[47] Engel's story questions the ethics of witness and exposure. In contrast, Carlos's singing of "The Tree" responds to Clorox's monologue with a happy-ending message of hope, as indicated by the omission of Curtis M.'s original adjective, "hopeless," from the song title. In the song, the morning after the fog, rather than the following Sunday, produces a scene of miraculous visibility. As the character Carlos sweetly sings: "Right there for all to see / Way up on a bough / Small and weak but hanging on somehow / Is a baby apple now."[48] Speeding up the timeline of the original tale, the song replaces Curtis M.'s delays and deferrals with immediacy of access—"Right there for all to see . . . now." In Holt's version, hope depends on visibility, such that the fog serves primarily as a dramatic contrast to a final unveiling.

"The Tree" favors the showing and telling of truth, as if to reassure Clorox and his peers that good will come from simply continuing to give voice to their thoughts and feelings, preferably in the presence of adults. By extension, the musical's white adult creators could appear as recruiting "children's voices from the ghetto" out of a fetishized obscurity and into a heroic grand reveal, presenting the truth of minority youth "for all to see." The song thus borders on advocating the kind of harvesting protested by Curtis M., like Shel Silverstein. But the double provision of song and written text, played out against the writers' absence from the theater, clouds any attempt to close in on a single, transparent truth. This conflict between the promise of access and its abeyance, parallel to the parading of young authors versus their absence, structures the drama of youth writing in *The Me*.

Curtis M. thus joins in absentia a tradition of resistance to racialized exposure in African American literature and theatrical performance. In the aesthetic tactic that Daphne Brooks terms "spectacular opacity," Black women performers paradoxically shroud themselves through acts of display, which "contest the 'dominative imposition of transparency' systemically willed on to black figures."[49] Translated from Brooks's study of nineteenth-century Black women performers to the context of multiracial, mostly boy writers in *The Me*, the concept of "spectacular opacity" enables a rereading of the title of both anthology and musical, "the me nobody knows." Despite its first person, the title does not come from any of children's own words in the anthology but was presumably invented by Joseph or his publishers. The appealingly vague phrase seems to advertise privileged access to an intimate and authentic child self. The word *me*, as a grammatical object, suggests the perspective of others looking at *me*, while also evoking the preference for *me* over *I* conventionally associated with child speakers. The question remains whether some "me nobody knows" does reveal itself to audiences or whether they instead experience a persistent unknowing. Curtis M.'s disruption of transparency, along with Akmir-U-Akbar's play of haunting absence and C. R.'s cultivation of relationships across distance, suggests that the position of "the me nobody knows" holds its own power. These young writers exercise inventive means to extend their influence, both answering the call for intimacy and veiling its terms.

MEETING THEIR MAKERS: CHARACTERIZATION, CASTING, AND WRITERS' RETURN

Curtis M.'s version of "spectacular opacity" prompts attention to what *The Me* does and does not display. The musical makers turn writers into characters and writing into drama. The resulting show harks back to young authors' bodies and identities even while distancing them by reassigning texts to characters formulated and cast by white adults. Ideas about gender and race charge characterization and casting in *The Me*. If, as Brian Herrera has argued, the "apparatus of casting reveals the inequitable operation of power always at play in the making of performance," then *The Me*'s adult-directed translations from writers to character roles to cast members can uncover how age, class, and race inequality structure the production.[50]

Will Holt's first draft of the script sheds light on the adult adapters' process of character assignment. The draft "Cast of Characters" lists twelve roles without names, identified only by age, race, and gender, such as "14 year old black girl" and "16 year old white boy." The list alternates "boy" and "girl" to end up with six parts of each, matching the gender breakdown of the final musical. Only after pasting most of the anthology texts in place do the adapters begin assigning pieces of dialogue, using pink pen to add names—not yet of characters but of actors, some of whom have presumably already been recruited.[51]

Although the musical is scripted for six boys and six girls, the words that constitute that script are pulled from a pool of mostly boy authors. In an approximate gender breakdown of the contributions to the original anthology, I count eighty-one male-authored texts, nineteen female-authored texts, fourteen texts that are either initialed or unsigned but contained male-identifying language, and thirty-six texts that are initialed or unsigned with no obvious gendering. Even accounting for error, these numbers indicate the predominance of male contributors in the anthology. Moreover, even in the more evenly gendered scripting of the musical, male characters voice the majority of lengthy and complex monologues in the show.[52]

Why did the musical makers seek to impose gender balance on *The Me*? They may have been responding to feminist influence and growing efforts to increase equity within the theater industry.[53] Published production notes by Martha Knight, the original stage manager of the show, indicate a second motive. Regarding costuming, she advises that "some of the girls do wear pants—but some skirts are necessary to make it look right."[54] Knight here evokes a professional theatrical standard of taste that is inherently normative—*looking right*—and that calls for a particular level of conventionally female-gendered presence. The rationale for this gender standard closely resembles discourses of race in casting. John Simon of *New York* magazine uses the same language as Knight to scorn the casting of Black actors in traditionally white roles in the mid-1960s New York Shakespeare Festival: "It is not only aurally that Negro actors present a problem; they *do not look right* in parts that historically demand white performers."[55] Only a few years later, the notoriously scathing Simon would become one of *The Me*'s most glowing champions, raising the question of what about the show suited his idea of good taste. The standard of *looking right*, moreover, clashes with the tone of many of the youth writings used in *The Me*, which focus on what is *wrong* with American life.

The showmakers' investment in displaying gendered rightness sheds light on the shifting racial assignments of the cast. In his anthology introduction, editor Joseph characterizes the contributors as "most[ly] . . . Black or Puerto Rican," while his anthology subtitle, "Children's Voices from the Ghetto," also indicates a specific demographic.[56] In turn, the creators of the musical designated parts for eight Black, two white, and two Puerto Rican roles, some of which had already been cast, as indicated by the pink-penned actors' names in the draft script. By the show premiere, those numbers had shifted to eight Black characters and four white characters, with the latter group including one "white (Puerto Rican)," Carlos, originally played by the Cuban-born Fernandez. Despite these definite racial assignments, Knight's production notes assure that "this number is not sacred; however, the ghetto is primarily black and Spanish. With a little thought and taste, you could change a few speeches when necessary to accommodate color."[57] This statement of flexibility nods to the growing trend of "race-blind" casting, related to the kind of nontraditional casting that John Simon resists. Rather than enabling additional casting of minority actors, however, Knight's assessment makes room for an increase in white cast members. Since no speeches in *The Me* are about whiteness, "chang[ing] a few speeches" would most likely serve to accommodate white actors.[58] Knight's *however* sets his caution that "the ghetto is primarily black and Spanish" against the flexibility of casting, as if changing the racial numbers of the cast would always involve fewer, not more, Black and Latinx roles. The appeal to "taste," while perhaps intended to prevent racially insensitive stumbles, recalls the language of *looking right*.

The changes to racialized casting in *The Me* hinged on the original pair of Puerto Rican roles, which shifted to an additional white role and the "white (Puerto Rican)" role of Carlos. Whether they failed to find conventionally legible Puerto Rican identity in the anthology, were swayed in the casting process, or wished to avoid association with *West Side Story*, the showmakers ultimately minimized Puerto Rican authorial presence. *The Me* thus followed a historical pattern by which, as Herrera states, US theater's gestures of Latinx representation only "rehears[e] audiences and actors in the spectacular notion that Latino cultural influence is new, Latino cultural forms are foreign, and Latinos themselves do not yet fit within US cultural systems."[59] In casting *The Me*, the issue is less the allowance of white cast members than the construction of whiteness as a default and a necessity, even as minority children remain central to the show's novel appeal. Racial and ethnic identity here risk becoming arbitrary markers of ethnographic verisimilitude, like costumes, threatening to defuse writers' critiques of the racial and ethnic systemization of poverty and ghettoization.

The "look" of *The Me* onstage thus became charged with the tensions of adaptation across race, class, gender, and age. Adult musical makers' reimagining of young writers' bodies according to a desired onstage aesthetic heightened the tension between young writers' roles as authors and characters. In turn, the young actors who moved, monologued, danced, and sang on *The Me* stage can be imagined as embodying the absently present, palimpsestic representation of young writers—even while amplifying their literary works.

Some writers did claim their place in the musical and publicly saw for themselves "what would become of" their words. Jerry Parker's February 1971 *Newsday* article reports on the "special authors' night" that invited writers of *The Me* to view the show and meet its cast.[60] Parker's account signals the stakes of writers' distance from their textual paths but also reveals how some writers asserted their presence, as living authors commenting on the frozen moment of their published childhood texts.

Writers' contact with the musical carried material consequences. According to Parker: "All of the authors are to share in the profits of the show according to the amount of material they contribute to it. Money is being held in trust for those who have not been found. Craig Stewart, 13, one of the four lyricists of 'Fugue for Four Girls[,]' has received $70 so far and has put it all in the bank 'to be used in the future, I don't know for what yet.'"[61] Parker's interest in Craig Stewart's banking efforts suggests the potential charm of this profit-sharing system. Joseph and his publisher, as the collectors of previously unpublished and unregistered work, likely possessed the full rights to license such adaptations of the anthology as *The Me* musical, owing the writers nothing, with the possible exception of What's Happening members. Joseph possibly stipulated small royalties for young writers as part of the contract for licensing the musical adaptation. I have found no evidence of whether he did the same for anthology profits; this practice was not uncommon among youth anthology editors. The separate system of musical royalties for youth writers may have assuaged adults' conscience and perhaps enhanced the liberal moralization of the musical without placing youth authorship on par with that of adults. As Jack Stillinger has pointed out, plays, unlike films, are customarily identified by and credited to their writers, rather than directors.[62] For example, earlier in this chapter, I referred to *The Me*'s musical rival as "Stephen Sondheim's *Company*"—giving the possessive to the writer, with no mention of the director or other collaborators. The issue of authors' credit and profit, then, carries special weight in the case of a theatrical production. *The Me* musical is primarily attributed to Gary William Friedman for music and Will Holt for lyrics, whether or not young writers collected their allotted share.

Those writers who did attend the "special authors' night" made their presence into a performance of its own. Bringing along "more than 100 friends and relatives," the writers filled in the numbers of their absent peers. In their new position as show watchers and listeners, the writers resembled critics—a parallel registered by Parker as he records writer Benjamin Warrick's take on the musical: "'I think it was dynamite,' he said, 'I liked the actors, they made it seem really realistic,' an appraisal very close to what most critics have had to say about the show."[63] Though minimally quoted by Parker, the writers' observing, evaluating stance at the authors' night asserted their ability to talk back to the performance.

Warrick's actor-focused comment also suggests a potential bond between writers and cast members. Two photos in Parker's article capture the charge of the live meeting between these two sets of young artists joined by adult collaborators (fig. 5). In the first picture, understudy Edloe looks up sweetly at writer Walter Perkins and holds up the Pepsi that he sips from a straw. In the second photo, writer Harry Wescott, explains the caption, "has other performers pointed out to him by Irene Cara who sings his number in the show." Delicately holding a hot dog in one hand, Wescott lifts his chin and surveys the room in the direction of Cara's gesture. In each image, a female actor plays smiling host(ess) to a male writer a head taller, who coolly inhabits his role as guest. The photographer uses gender to reinforce the perception of a generic difference between cast members and writers. At the same time, the images suggest a dynamic of mutual influence: while writers have supplied actors with lyrics and jobs, actors now serve as guides to the resulting theatrical world. The writers' presence stands analogously to memory or time travel, since the authors' night took place years after the composition of the original texts. Rhonda Peterson, for instance, wrote her anthologized work at age seven and attended the musical at age eleven. By meeting the actors who voice their past words, the young-yet-older writers seem to encounter a version of their younger, more childlike selves. The documentation of this meeting enables an imagining of an artistic alliance or affinity between young writers and actors, with the latter taking up writers' words from adult collaborators and giving them newly youth-authored voice and meaning. The potential for alliance between writers and actors is especially powerful given the continued influence of many of *The Me* actors. Four of the original stars moved straight from *The Me* to regular roles on *The Electric Company*, the older-kid version of *Sesame Street*; several cast members, such as Hattie Winston and Irene Cara, continue to conduct successful singing and acting careers today—perhaps carrying some piece of *The Me Nobody Knows* writers with them. At least one writer used the special authors' night to intervene in the media narrative about his work. Harry Wescott, featured in the second photo, has the last words in Parker's article: "And there is Harry Wescott, 17, of Harlem, who stopped writing poetry two years ago, but said after hearing his words . . . that his muse had been stirred anew. 'It was so beautiful,' he said, 'to know people were listening. I'll probably write some more now.'"[64] Wescott suggests his

Newsday Photos by Dick Morseman

Above, cast member Edloe and author Walter Perkins get acquainted at the party after the performance. Right, lyric writer Harry Wescott has other performers pointed out to him by Irene Cara who sings his number in the show.

FIGURE 5. The "special authors' night" as featured in Jerry Parker, "Gathering the 'Me' Almost Nobody Knew," *Newsday*, February 22, 1971. Photographs by Dick Morseman. © 1971 Newsday. All rights reserved. —Used under license.

openness toward the voicing of his words by a young girl, a scripting that typifies the gender dynamics of the musical adaptation. The character Lillie Mae, described in the "Character Breakdown" of the script as aged ten or eleven, is one of the youngest in the ensemble but, as played by Irene Cara, was also one of the most charismatic and praised roles in the production. Wescott also takes a positive view of the ambiguous treatment of his poem in the show. Lillie Mae recites from Wescott's lyric in the dream collage that opens the musical, as characters hold the spotlight one by one:

> Windy windy windy skys
> deep blue fallen over my eyes.
> The birds so loud and clear
> as if you feel a soft hand
> in the air.[65]

Wescott's spell-like poem blurs the line between the real and imagined, helping to enchant audiences into temporarily accepting a stage as their reality. But when Lillie Mae next tries to resume the thought later in the scene, venturing, "Windy windy windy skies . . ." she is interrupted by "[ALL:] Shut up."[66] Wescott nevertheless insists to Parker that "people were listening" and are ready for an encore. Wescott's evaluation of "so beautiful" may apply not only to his experience of the musical but also to his poetry itself. He thus gently pushes back on the adult scripting of his lyric to uphold its aesthetic quality and strong reception. The casual remark that "I'll probably write some more now" claims his sure ability to replicate his success, even as he ages out of the literary brand of childhood.

In his blithe confidence, does Wescott defiantly court skepticism? He and his peers at the special authors' night would have known the racialized processes of cultural consumption that powered their spotlight and that fellow writer Corbin would name from Brandeis a year later. Bleakly prescient of the entrenchment of structural racism in the 1980s, Corbin declares: "This country's just about ready to turn its back on the blacks. We was given a chance to be heard. We were noted. But now the time has come to turn us back into niggers again."[67] Corbin's sardonic emphasis on the temporariness of attention, as Black youth are ushered on and then off the stage of national attention, could describe the passing nature of a Broadway show or a young person's aging out of American cultural indulgence for children. Corbin marks the material realities behind The Me and its special authors' night. He makes clear that the same cultural production that focused attention on marginalized young people could also obscure them.

Child authors like C. R., Akmir-U-Akbar, and Curtis M. critique and manage this double-edged cultural spotlight by leveraging the disembodied nature of their writings, a tactic heightened by the reembodied performance of The Me. As Wescott and Corbin demonstrate, however, young authors also exercise their agency in embodied ways, refusing to conveniently disappear. The writers of The Me Nobody Knows invent tools of both absence and presence to ensure that, to follow Akmir-U-Akbar's pen-hero, the hands that reshape their stories "shall be guided by me."

CHAPTER 4

"Criticism Is Out of the Question"
The Adult Reception of Children's Writing

STUDENT: Well, I knew that everybody might be a little shocked by what Juan read. But I got the feeling that maybe nobody really heard Juan, really heard him when he was reading.

AUDIENCE: What do you mean we didn't hear?

STUDENT: I don't think it really went in.

AUDIENCE: Do you think we would have booed if we had heard it?

STUDENT: No, I don't mean that.

AUDIENCE: This was very moving poetry.

STUDENT: There was no reaction in your faces. That's what I was looking for. . . . I just wanted somebody to look at Juan and say, "Well," or something. You just looked like blank faces that couldn't hear. . . . People just seemed to sit there, and I was curious. Could they really hear?

The tense exchange in this chapter's epigraph over "what Juan read" took place between an unidentified student from Philadelphia's all-Black Simon Gratz High School and an audience of education professionals and academics, likely majority white, at a 1969 Lehigh University conference.[1] Organized by Nancy Larrick, best known for her 1965 article "The All-White World of Children's Literature," and attended by many other prominent education scholars, the "Poetry Festival" likely featured few youth-participatory elements other than the panel of Simon Gratz students and teachers.

In the wake of Juan's reading of his provocative poem about "whitie," Juan's unnamed peer (hereafter referred to as "Juan's peer" or "JP") wonders if "maybe nobody really heard Juan." One can imagine the decorous silence that apparently greeted Juan's performance, whether stemming from academic etiquette, discomfort, or disapproval of the anti-"whitie" poem. Cutting this quiet, JP calls out the audience's absence of meaningful response: "nobody really heard Juan. . . . You just looked like blank faces." By scrutinizing the audience's affect as if they were the performers, JP calls out listeners for consuming young poets' voices while giving nothing back. Four repetitions of "really" contest interpersonal unreality, the feeling that others' thoughts and experiences do not truly alter one's own perceptual world. JP, in contrast, seems to speak from a definite vision of what *real* literary response should look like. Declaring, "I just wanted someone to look at Juan," JP triangulates themself, Juan, and the audience in a geometry of response. Though later published under the title "Straight Talk from Teenagers," the Simon Gratz panel transcript is a record of teenaged talk that is not "straight" but rather shaped like a boomerang, designed to venture out and be returned. Amid a sea of adult-authored academic papers about children, the student asserts that adults' reception is, in turn, received.

JP's commentary highlights circa-1970 young authors' investment in the readership of their texts. The young writers discussed in the preceding chapters not only questioned but also found ways to intervene in the reception of their work, from the Voice of the Children poets (chapter 1), who solicited adult help with spelling and grammar "because they wanted to make sure that what they said could not be mistaken, by anybody," to C. R.'s fascination with "what would become of" his writing (chapter 3).[2] Children's keen observation of their own reception constitutes a "cognizan[ce] of the institutions of criticism," as Mike Sell identifies in avant-garde literary movements, including Black Arts.[3] By producing texts that stretch the limits of criticism and finding ways to intervene in and critique the processes of reception and interpretation, circa-1970 young writers invite questions about the very definition of literature, how it should be evaluated, and what it should do in the world.

By interrogating their own position and unsettling the position of their readers, children disrupt what Jodi Melamed has identified as the liberal moralization of "reading literature as a way for dominant classes to come to know racialized others intimately." The very act of reading and interpreting texts, Melamed argues, has served as a practice for entrenching US racial order: determining acceptable narratives of difference and processing these narratives as a source of white enlightenment that elides the radical content of anti-racism and leaves racial capitalism intact.[4] While Melamed, Roderick Ferguson, and other scholars center the university, particularly English and literature programs, as a key site of manufacture of racial order, I argue that this process of racialization has also taken place in post-1965 children's literacies—both adult-shaped literature for young readers and adult-shaped opportunities for child authorship. Circa-1970 youth writing illustrates how the practice of reading racial order into existence can be both enforced and contested in arenas outside of the academy, and specifically in children's culture.

In Melamed's periodization, the late 1960s mark the twilight of racial liberalism, with its insistence on white benevolence through the incorporation of racial difference into US capitalist democracy. In the following decades, radical movements of the 1960s and 1970s would be co-opted into liberal multiculturalism, which presented acceptable strains of multicultural narrative to accredit white students as enlightened consumers "in (the spirit of) antiracist activism" without its change-making substance.[5] Somewhat ahead of Melamed's timeline, I find that this process of liberal co-optation is already underway in the reception of circa-1970 youth writing. White-dominated adult critical discourse perceives children's texts as authentic, individualistic, and identity-based narratives of difference, making illegible these texts' relationships to radical movements. Juan's peer challenges this illegibility by refusing to let a majority-white adult audience feast on children's words in peace. The example of JP reveals how this generation of young writers observed and critiqued a nascent form of liberal multiculturalism.

This chapter follows children's lead in scrutinizing adults, particularly the largely white and middle-class critics and educators who published their responses to youth anthologies in popular and scholarly periodicals. As youth anthologies increased in number and prominence, adult readers struggled to find critical footing. What aspects of youth anthologies should be interpreted, what context about the children and their collaborators mattered, and what distinguished a "bad" anthology from a "good" one? Adults' vexed, ambivalent responses to children's writings both productively unsettled the waters of literary culture and muddled public understanding of the texts themselves. At best, children's writings provoked adults to rethink literary value, authorial agency, and anti-racist affect. More often, critics resorted to a set of rhetorical moves that replaced true interpretation with backhanded praise. Planting doubts about the literary validity of children's texts even in gestures of approval, circa-1970 critics set up youth anthologies to fall into obscurity. This chapter identifies interpretive pitfalls that twenty-first-century adults might try to avoid ourselves, in our approach to both historical and contemporary youth-authored texts. I then return to the work of poet, theorist, and youth writing collaborator June Jordan to locate an alternative spirit of interpretation, rooted in an ethic of interpersonal connection and transformation.

YOUTH WRITING MEETS THE NEW CRITICS

Circa-1970 adult reviewers of youth writing were steeped in the paradigms of racial liberalism and New Criticism. It is no wonder that these critics struggled to interpret children's work given that the dominant literary critical framework was explicitly defined against the writing of schoolchildren. In their landmark 1946 essay "The Intentional Fallacy," which advances one of the best-known tenets of New Criticism, W. K. Wimsatt, Jr., and M. C. Beardsley set the bounds of proper interpretation:

> The art of inspiring poets, or at least of inciting something like poetry in young persons, has probably gone further in our day than ever before. Books of creative writing such as those issued from the Lincoln School are interesting evidence of what a child can do if taught how to manage himself honestly. All this, however, would appear to belong to an art separate from criticism, or to a discipline which one might call the psychology of composition, valid and useful, an individual and private culture, yoga, or system of self-development which the young poet would do well to notice, but different from the public science of evaluating poems.[6]

The mention of the Lincoln School here references Hughes Mearns's popular 1925 book *Creative Youth*, in which the progressive educator, credited with coining the phrase "creative writing," details his methods for inspiring schoolchildren's literary production and collects the resulting child-authored works. Wimsatt and Beardsley use the figure of the Lincoln School child to disavow the connection between literary inspiration and interpretation, strengthening the essay's argument against attention to authorial intention.[7] Children's writing is relegated to the same category as exoticized "yoga" and, prior to what I have quoted here, an ironic discussion of whether poetry writing improves after drinking beer. What the child produces is merely "something like poetry," a kind of facsimile that can be "incit[ed]," like an illusion at a magic show. Portraying poetic inspiration as childlike and suspect provides a useful foil for the mature and masculine "science" of textual interpretation. Children's writings constantly remind adult readers of the

physical human bodies and concrete circumstances behind literary production, raising questions about agency and intention. This tendency threatens
the New Critical concept of textual objectivity, the apprehension of a text as
a standalone package of meaning. Dispensing with children's writing serves
Wimsatt and Beardsley's purpose of refuting the intentional fallacy.

It is fitting, then, that attention to children's writings surged in the late
1960s moment of increasing contestation of New Criticism. The growing
body of anti-racist and feminist literary criticism and theory, radical artists'
scorn for "academic poets," and the popularization of reader-response theory,
among other critical directions, was weakening the universal hold of Wimsatt, Beardsley, and company. Black Arts artists and critics "sought aesthetic
situations that explicitly rejected the object as such and the objectivity that
separated the viewer from the viewed," in a direct contradiction of New
Critical terms.[8] Live poetry readings fueled a growing commitment to literature as performed and shaped in interaction with the audience, in contrast
to the New Critical conception of autonomous textual meaning. Change-
making adults saw education and children's writing as a powerful site for
remaking the cultural relationship to literature and language. As Philip
Lopate recounts, youth writing advocates "diagnosed an alienating separation
between standard English as it was taught and the language people actually
spoke and used for communication; they saw a rusting of the tools of language, partly as a result of the influence of public speech."[9] Children offered
the opportunity to start afresh, revitalizing language with the help of the
right literacy pedagogy. Whereas Wimsatt and Beardsley use the figure of
the child writer as a tool of differentiation, to delineate the bounded space of
criticism, Lopate recalls a turn to children as agents of reconnection. As adult
readers encountered the wave of circa-1970 youth anthologies, the figure of
the child writer was transforming, unevenly and incompletely, from literary
and linguistic threat to savior.

In response to these contradictory concepts, critics alternately advocated
exclusion and inclusion of children's writing from the category of true literature. Education scholar Patrick Groff carries the flag of exclusion in a 1966
Horn Book diatribe. Groff scorns "a most curious practice . . . [of] teaching
children to write poetry before they have had opportunities to truly learn
about it." Allowing children to attempt poetry without proper training, Groff
asserts, has loosed a "flood of execrable doggerel." More seriously, for Groff,
this phenomenon threatens to accelerate "the seeming downward plunge

of the status of poetry" in culture at large. Groff bases his criticism in an argument about the definition of true poetry, which "transcends the literal meaning of expository writing" and "is not translatable into prose."[10] In the tradition of Wimsatt and Beardsley—but, remarkably, in the context of scholarship on children's education—Groff relies on children's writings negatively to define true poetry. Determined to defend both children and poetry, Groff seems to fear their mixing, as if defending children against themselves.

Such takedowns invited other adults to take on the role of defending champions. B. Jo Kinnick and Peter Neumeyer exemplify the move of inclusion, striving to prove the qualification of children's writing according to common literary standards. In her review of *I Heard a Scream in the Street* for *English Journal*, Kinnick answers her own question "How good are the [children's] poems as poetry?" with a textbook checklist: "By Laurence Perrine's guidelines, the level [of poetic quality] is high. 'Honesty, courage, humility' all are here. 'Central purpose?' Indeed. 'Excess or inexact words?' Few. 'Clashes between sound and sense?' No. Rather the closest affinity."[11] Kinnick's turn to Perrine, whose ubiquitous literature textbooks drew on New Critical predecessors, demonstrates the drive to gain child writers entry into an existing literary club.

Neumeyer's more involved assessment of *The Voice of the Children* in the *Teachers College Record* further advances this inclusionary project. He frames his review around two questions: "Problem one: Shall this art be regarded somehow differently for having been produced by Jane and John, *age ten*? Problem two: Shall we judge a political or exhortatory art by normal aesthetic standards, or shall we say, 'No, given the crisis this art has sprung from, normal aesthetic standards are beside the point'?" *The Voice of the Children* wins praise by persuading Neumeyer to answer *no* to the first question and *the former* to the second: children's writing, in this view, should not be read differently in light of the author's age and should be evaluated by "normal aesthetic standards." Neumeyer's repetition of *normal* makes his priorities clear. His advocacy of children's writing adheres to New Critical ways of reading. He praises two poems in *The Voice of the Children* as "the closest possible objective correlatives to the sensibilities of two poets," using T. S. Eliot's famous term. Neumeyer pays a similar compliment to the last line of a piece by young poet Michael Gill: "'Go to work, new critics,' one is tempted to say, 'show us some of the meanings.' What are the 'days of my people'?"[12] While open to young writers' literary value, Neumeyer is conservative in his reinforcement of a dominant interpretive framework and assimilationist approach to youth writing. In Groff, Kinnick, and Neumeyer alike, the common compulsion to pass judgment on children's writing, to justify it as literature or not, falls back on the very literary notions that 1960s–1970s cultural movements sought to dismantle.

(UN)CRITICAL MANEUVERS: HOW TO OBSCURE YOUTH WRITING

Most reviewers of circa-1970 youth writing anthologies avoid the direct question of their relationship to the conventional literary bookshelf. Still, the arguments of both Groff and Neumeyer circulate implicitly, sometimes in the same review, as if whispering into the critic's opposite ears. To reconcile the simultaneous impulses to endorse and to exclude the genre, reviewers resort to a set of rhetorical maneuvers that manage readerly tensions and uncertainties about youth writing without truly engaging in critical interpretation. Namely, reviewers distinguish between the emotional and formal qualities of youth writing, make moral exhortations, disavow criticism, focus on adult collaborators, invent metaphors of child-adult collaboration, and manage writers' anti-racist affects. Identifying these six maneuvers in the reception of circa-1970 youth writing may help present-day adult readers avoid the same mistakes.

Separating Feeling and Form

Critics attempt to make youth writing approachable by separating its content from its style. Ruth Kearney Carlson demonstrates this tactic in the journal *Elementary English*: "At present thousands of children in various schools of the United States are expressing themselves with emotion or feeling, but rarely does their poetry reflect poetic techniques which interrelate Art and Humanity." This idea of feeling over form appears even in glowing praise of youth writing. *New York Magazine* theater critic John Simon promises in his show-making review of *The Me Nobody Knows* musical, "[T]hough the words are often ill-fitting or threadbare, their actuality and ability to move you are supreme." Similarly, in the *Chicago Tribune*, William Leonard deems the children's words in *The Me* "sometimes only semi-literate," yet somehow affecting, "definitely the heart of the whole thing."[13] By advancing contrasting assessments of feeling and form, critics reconcile their simultaneous allegiance and aversion to child-authored art.[14]

Children's poetry advocate Myra Cohn Livingston, who sparred with Patrick Groff in defense of children's authorship, sheds light on adults' quest for emotional content in children's work. The investment in child writers' "feeling," Livingston suggests, may register the growing "complaint that New Critical interpretation divested literary communication of personal feeling," resulting in "a kind of depersonalization and dehumanization of the experience of reading." This sentiment is tied to white-authored stereotypes of non-white emotional authenticity, for it is "the recently published writing of ghetto children" that reveals children's "true emotions and feelings," which may allow all readers "to recognize that Puritanical strictures on human emotions *must* go." Even as Livingston aims to defend children's writings, she undermines them by separating their feeling and form, urging teachers to "permit these children to express themselves in whatever form of language they can."[15] Livingston thus aligns with her antagonist Groff, who concludes a review of one 1972 classroom anthology: "In short, these are not all remarkable bits of literature by children. Nonetheless they should serve the function of dissuading the prevalent attitude that poor, nonwhite children have nothing of significance to say."[16] Framed dubiously in the negative, Groff's weighing of "literature" against "significance" frankly reveals the raced and classed character of the distinction between form and feeling.

Reviewers thus fall into the interpretive trap censured by Susan Sontag, whose 1966 essay "Against Interpretation" notes "the frequency with which quite admirable works of art are defended as good although what is miscalled their style is acknowledged to be crude or careless." Such an approach creates a gap in critics' ability to explain the quality of a work, and conversely, to justify the importance of style if a text can apparently, to quote John Simon, "move you . . . supreme[ly]" without it.[17] Though critics consistently associate youth writing anthologies with the impulse for social change, they seem unable to take up this change as readers, interpreting children's work with conservative, increasingly challenged frameworks. In part, this pattern reflects the tendency of children's culture to retain discarded and expired material, as when children continue to sing rhymes with antique and disturbing lyrics.[18] But in their very zeal to distinguish feeling from form and to explain their mixed feelings about youth writing, perhaps critics were knocking at the door of a different mode of reading, one that they sensed around them but had not yet fully apprehended.

Moralizing

The endorsements of white experts on the book jacket of *The Voice of the Children* exemplify the tendency to replace criticism with moral imperatives. The strident blurbs present youth poetry as indispensable without actually identifying its content. The editors promise "[a] voice which must be heard"; Nancy Larrick insists, "Theirs is a poetry no one can afford to miss"; and fellow education professor Charles F. Reasoner warns, "If we do not hear it, then it is we—not they—who are incoherent."[19] Reasoner raises the specter of a kind of moral curse on the uncomprehending, as if young writers' texts might leave older readers robbed of their own voices. These adult-directed urgings ignore the possibility of young readers of the anthology, even though Holt, Rinehart and Winston published the book within its school division.

Reviewers of *The Me* musical share this bias toward hyperbolic acclaim and universal demands. The notoriously scathing Simon titles his column "The 'Me' You Must Get to Know" and finds the show "so good that if every legislator and slum landlord were to see it—and since it should be seen by everybody, that includes those unsavory professions—it might put an end to ghettos." Simon's blatantly unrealistic promise and uncharacteristically universalizing declarations cast a pall of irony over his endorsement. At the *Village Voice*, Martin Washburn seconds the motion: "Attendance at 'The Me Nobody Knows' should be compulsory for the Board of Education. Everyone else will want to go." Bob Micklin's contribution to the show's "unanimous critical acclaim" in *Newsday* borders on threat: "Everybody doesn't like something, but nobody doesn't like 'The Me Nobody Knows.'"[20] These critics prescribe the show like a medicine, giving the concept of "must-see" an anxious intensity.

The overt illogic of Micklin's statement indicates how moralizing children's writing as a universal good stymies analysis, resulting in an almost studiously uncritical mode. Reviewers seem determined to answer children's perceived unintellectual emotionality with their own unthinking feelings. Leonard, for instance, discards journalistic skepticism with almost gleeful abandon: "You have to believe these words, for they actually were written by children of New York City's ghetto—and children of one big city ghetto are like children of any other."[21]

This atmosphere of critical peer pressure drew occasional protests. Reviewing his local production of *The Me* for the *Washington Post*, Richard Coe comments sardonically on the trend: "It would take a sadist of clinical viciousness to breathe an unkind thought about 'The MNK,' but I also find it impossible to go along with the 'stunned' New York notices which find this an 'unforgettable joy' and other such encomiums."[22] Coe locates the aggression under the surface of endorsements of *The Me*. What Coe seems to miss is that empty applause and stubborn suspicion are two sides of the same uncritical coin, working to exclude children's writings from substantive consideration.

Abstention

Critics' breathless moralization often slide into full abandonment of the critical act. Washburn, for instance, facetiously throws up his hands to conclude his *The Me* review: "Who knows? If we let them [children] have their say, maybe they'll go to bed on time." Even Eve Merriam, a daring and politically radical children's author, ends her review of *The Voice of the Children* with a loss of words: "One can only echo what June Jordan states in her Afterword: 'With all my heart, I wish the voices of these children peace and power.'"[23] While I sympathize with Merriam's sentiment about June Jordan's words, the purpose of a review is to offer fresh and deepened assessment. Critics famed for their sharp takes struggle to provide children this respect.

Edith Oliver concludes her *New Yorker* review of *The Me*: "Criticism is out of the question. How is it possible to *think* anything about 'The Me Nobody Knows'?"[24] Known as a tough but open-minded champion of new playwrights, Oliver offers damning praise. By denying the ability to think about children's writings, she feeds into the narratives of impossibility that elide young people of color and their aesthetic acts. Oliver's use of the passive voice emphasizes her abstention from thought in a strangely double declaration, which could be paraphrased as "consideration is not up for consideration."

Perhaps white critics shrunk from intellectual criticism in part out of deference to the era's anti-racist critiques of white Western norms of aesthetic value and rational thought. This reasoning, however, would rest on misreadings of anti-racist critique and of youth writing. The refusal to critique children's writings also elides the function of those writings *as* critique. To declare "criticism out of the question" is to distance the anti-racist, change-making work of children's writings. Critics' abstention comes too close to calling up the ghost of Thomas Jefferson's racist response to the work of Phillis Wheatley: "The compositions published under her name are below the dignity of criticism."[25] The pattern of underresponse toward child writers, and Black and Puerto Rican child writers in particular, suggests the breadth of the problem that JP calls out: "I just wanted somebody to look at Juan and say, 'Well,' or something."

Crediting Adults

In an ancillary move of critical avoidance, reviewers dedicate their discussions to the details of adult collaboration rather than children's actual texts.

The marketing and critical reception of youth anthologies of the era often focus on what teachers have *drawn from* or *cultivated in* students, positioning teachers as subjects and child writers as objects. Write-ups of youth anthologies commonly begin with a substantial description of adult collaborators' strategies and end with quotes from children's writings, minimizing commentary on the texts themselves.[26] Even James Baldwin, a steady advocate for the young whose interest in youth writing is discussed further in this book's epilogue, praises a classroom anthology primarily in the terms of adult actions: "And the teacher, who no longer was a teacher, made a compilation of the poetry these kids wrote and he let them talk. He respected them. He dealt with them as though they were—and in fact as all children are, as all human beings are—a kind of miracle. And because he did that, something happened."[27] As Baldwin's account suggests, the details of adult work may guide future collaborations with children and, more generally, inspire hope in education and social change. This interpretive approach, however, can credit collaborators with children's textual results. It is difficult to imagine an equivalent treatment of adult writing, in which the book would be reviewed entirely by describing the strategies of the author's mentors and editors.

Critics both applaud adults' ability to unlock child truth and insist on these collaborators' lack of undue influence, as demonstrated by several examples from the influential education journal *Elementary English*. In a review of *The Me Nobody Knows*, Jane D. Vreeland declares that editor Stephen Joseph "must have earned the trust of the children, or they would not have shared their personal thoughts with a teacher. Their writing has not been corrected, it is truly the authors.'"[28] Vreeland is speculating here: Joseph's anthology introduction says little about his editing process, and, as I discuss in chapter 3, Joseph did not know all of the children featured in his collection. For Vreeland, the texts' deviations from standard spelling and grammar attest to adult collaborators' light touch. Mary Anne Hall and Linda B. Gambrell similarly report on *The Voice of the Children*: "No discipline of form was imposed, resulting in poetry and prose of intense honesty and insight." Adults receive credit for the "result[s]" of children's writing, but in the passive form of strategic inaction and wise restraint.[29]

In the early 1970s, *Elementary English* featured a regular column of children's writing, "The Children's Page." Column editor Jean McClellan demonstrates the impulse simultaneously to celebrate and to contain adult collaborators' role in her policies for submissions to the column:

1. Classroom work is submitted by the teacher.
2. It is original.
3. The student's work has not been altered, other than spelling or punctuation corrections. We're interested in *children's* work.[30]

McClellan's policies emphasize the value of unmediated originality, even
as the requirement of teacher submission, as well as McClellan's own role as
editor, depends on mediation. The publication of guidelines almost one year
into the column's run suggests that McClellan had received submissions that
she deemed inappropriate or suspicious. Her declaration, "We're interested
in *children's* work," implies that some submissions were insufficiently child-
authored, raising the question of how that evaluation could be made. In both
reviews and solicitations of children's work, adults express simultaneous
enthusiasm and doubt about their own influence over youth writing.

Crafting Metaphors of Collaboration

Reviewers invent a colorful range of metaphors to imagine and express
anxiety about child-adult collaboration. Linnea Lilja characterizes youth as
"probably the most perishable of authors of today's world," often "bruis[ed]"
by adults' rigid rules or disinterest. Lilja's image of delicate fruit portrays
young writers as easily contaminated or brought to a hastened maturity.
Other metaphors suggest the elusive nature of adult collaboration. In a
column on *The Children: Poems and Prose from Bedford-Stuyvesant* for the
Arizona Republic, Willard Abraham credits teacher-editor Irving Benig for
"his success in unlocking some of the buried treasure in these neglected
children." Continuing this imagery of hiding, Kinnick describes teachers as
"shadowy figures in the wings," a phrase of praise that is nevertheless omi-
nous.[31] Images of hiding and revealing suggest that appreciation for adult
collaborators goes hand in hand with unease about the intangible space
between adult and child agency.

These images can veer into the weird and even uncanny. The title of one
article on youth writing by Teachers and Writers Collaborative director
Marvin Hoffman, "The Other Mouth: Writing in the Schools," draws on the
fantastical imagery of a writing prompt designed by Ron Padgett. Hoffman
reports how Padgett pitched his prompt to fifth graders:

You woke up this morning, remember? . . . Now, what if you had been rub-
bing the back of your neck and you feel something there and you run over

to the mirror and look back there and you see a tiny mouth in the back of your neck!! Where did it come from? What does it say to you? You can talk to it with your voice and mouth, and it seem to understand, because it answers you. It seems to know you. Now I want you to write a story or poem about this mouth. Or just tell me what it says.[32]

In keeping with his New York School affiliation, Padgett uses zaniness, randomness, and games to release children's unconscious inspiration. He describes his "tiny mouth" prompt as simply "interesting and fun" and thus successful with fifth graders. Yet the resemblance of the "tiny mouth in the back" to an anus joins the ample supply of sexual hints in adult images of youth writing, from bruised fruit to unlocked treasure. Entendres aside, Padgett offers a striking image of multivocality. The pairing of tiny mouth and main mouth seems to allegorize the collaboration of children and adults in literary production. This meaning remains unclear, however, because neither mouth fully aligns with the position of child writer or adult collaborator. The adjustment of Padgett's term, "the tiny mouth," to the title of Hoffman's article, "The Other Mouth," releases a new set of associations. Most immediately, the altered phrase suggests the strange otherness of one's own poetic voice. More deeply, the image of the other mouth as the voice in the back, an unsettling part of the larger body, evokes the rise of anti-racist literatures and the specter of the *other* in white America. The rogue mouth whispers of the link between adults' vexed responses to youth writing and the growing strength of minority literary movements. While sometimes troubling or at least misleading, metaphors of youth writing and collaboration can open up productive uncertainty, helping readers avoid snap judgments and remain imaginatively open to young writers' words.

Managing Anti-Racist Affect

Circa-1970 youth anthologies emerged at a moment of national debate over the tone and spirit of anti-racism and the uses of anti-racist anger. Young people participated in this conversation, in part through their writings. Critics attempt to summarize and manage young writers' anti-racist affects with a dichotomous pair of descriptors: *bitter* and *fresh*.

Bitter is one of the most frequently repeated terms in the reception of circa-1970 youth anthologies. Ruth Kearney Carlson demonstrates this widespread concern in her discussion of *The Voice of the Children*: "Some of the writing is beautiful, often the words are *bitterly* resentful, but these young poe[ts] express themselves in a clear, authentic style." Similarly, of reviewing five thousand child-authored poetry submissions for her anthology *I Heard a Scream in the Street*, Nancy Larrick recalls: "Again and again I found cries of loneliness and despair, but never any tributes to parents, friends, or teachers. School has evidently been a *bitter* experience for many of these children." Larrick does not discuss how the solicitation of writings by her and various teachers may have encouraged and selected for children's most "bitter" texts. The perception of bitterness spans literary forms and styles, as evidenced by Teachers & Writers Collaborative member Art Berger's explanation of comedy in his students' work: "This *bitter* humor is an attempt to deal with realities these children see and feel helpless to change."[33]

Bitterness names a way of reacting expressively to social conditions, a worldview developed through experience and thus potentially a way to take politics personally. By invoking bitterness, critics attempt to articulate the link between child writers' expressions of personal emotion and social critique. But the term can also euphemize or minimize radical rage. Describing child writers as bitter implicitly distances them from the politics of Martin Luther King, Jr., who frequently defined himself against bitterness: "And once more I caught myself and said: 'You must not allow yourself to become bitter.'"[34] This philosophy would not always hold in the activism of the Black Power years. References to the bitterness of Black and Latinx young writers are thus embedded in perceptions of anti-racist movements. Carlson makes this connection explicit in her discussion of youth texts that "reflect a bitter antagonism between a Black adolescent poetry and the white man" with language that might "disturb persons unfamiliar with the open language of ghetto youth who wish to debunk the pretentious, hypocritical ways of schools and society." Such poets, Carlson suggests, could learn from "primitive Eskimo and Nahuatl poets who looked for a world of beauty rather than one of junkies, garbage, poverty, and hatred between races. Some day the urban child of the ghetto may leave his despair and dark bitterness behind."[35] Using racial stereotypes of both black and Native artistic styles, Carlson typifies a common ambivalence in white-dominated publications toward young writers' affects. Adults perceive children's bitter writing as potentially providing an alternative to window-breaking, business-disrupting, or gun-toting forms of anti-racist action but also as potentially setting the stage for those forms. The label *bitter* can express either sympathy or suspicion, both marking and limiting young writers' power.

Young writers' bitter reputation holds both semantic and temporal complexity. *Bitter* can describe both the food being tasted and the person doing the tasting. According to this semantic slippage, swallowing bitter things can make one a bitter person. The label of youth writings as bitter may apply simultaneously to the writers' life experiences, their resulting perspectives, and the consequent experiences of youth anthology readers. This uncertainty regarding the bittering agent gives the term ambiguity, leaving in question the source of affect in children's writings. Are feelings taken to be the creative products of child writers or simply sociological evidence of environment and influence? Temporally, moreover, convention associates bitterness not with children but with old age, as in "bitter old man." Bitterness implies a posterior state, an effect of past experience. The characterization of child writers as bitter thus contradicts an idea with which it closely coexists: that child writers are valuable because they are *not yet* acculturated, calloused, or otherwise contaminated by the adult world.

This temporal paradox arises in the linked labels of *bitter* and *fresh*. Neumeyer, for instance, finds "such precision . . . such freshness" in *The Voice of the Children*.[36] The idealized child writer speaks with perceptual and moral *freshness* about the kinds of experiences and social realities that are thought to produce *bitterness* and cynicism. Innocence and experience meet in this popular construction of young people of color. Young writers thus risk disqualification from their position of cultural authority through their very success: if they can write such fresh testaments to oppression, then they must soon be turned bitter. In a 1972 dissertation surveying children's poetry, Catherine Mackintosh claims that "poetry of protest and poetry dealing with less attractive aspects of contemporary life . . . written by the young, though often formless and unpolished, has a spontaneity and freshness" but "is also apt to wither away."[37] Drawing on the tendency to read children's feeling over form, Mackintosh makes a somewhat self-fulfilling prediction of youth writing's lack of longevity. Mackintosh's assessment of what she euphemistically terms the "contemporary" demonstrates the deeply raced and classed nature of the discursive space between freshness and bitterness. Together and apart, these are catch-22 terms, in which young writers could capture public attention only temporarily and always at a cost.

While youth writing found occasional bold critics, perhaps most damaging were those disparagements wrapped in praise, which functioned to contain the texts' radical implications for literature, culture, politics, and social life in the US. The *containment* of youth writing, in fact, runs through all of the above (un)critical maneuvers: the separation of feeling and form, empty moralization, critical abdication, the crediting of adults, and anxious metaphors of agency. These habits also evince critics' impulse to rule on the authenticity of youth writing, both as children's real words and as real literature. The are-they-or-aren't-they approach to children's writings can flatten the expressiveness of these texts, reducing them to mere cries to be heard, worthy only in their very status as speech. May we readers of the twenty-first century monitor these tendencies within ourselves, even as we practice alternative ways of receiving children's words.

CRITICAL EMBARRASSMENT AND AN ALTERNATIVE READERLY ETHIC

I suspect one additional pattern of adult response played a role in youth writing's fall into obscurity. This last maneuver stems not from a lack of sensitivity but from an abundance of it: embarrassment. Readers may be embarrassed not by youth writing itself but by the missteps of surrounding adults, with their stereotypical and sentimental ways of treating young writers and their work. Even Phillip Lopate, a lifelong advocate of children's writing and playful examiner of adult collaborators' biases and foibles, is quick to distance himself from the politically unsavory aspects of the genre: "Certainly, the work in a book like *The Me Nobody Knows* is rather pedestrian and meager from the standpoint of language and imagination, yet it sold thousands of copies because it corresponded to a momentary hunger on the part of people, mostly white people, to hear deprived schoolchildren expressing—deprivation."[38] The belief that the publication of *The Me Nobody Knows* ultimately caused more harm than good seems to drive Lopate's dismissal of the texts within the anthology.

Far from superficial, this embarrassment is both intellectual—perceiving a lack of rigor and nuance—and political—fearing these texts' negative impact on the projects of racial and socioeconomic justice. Apparently tainted texts can trigger intellectual and political embarrassment that stops interpretation in its tracks, occluding insight. Perhaps the very critique of reception provided in this chapter risks further embarrassing present-day adult readers away from youth writing. *Receptive pessimism*—by which I mean the recognition of how easily one may read wrongly—is understandable given how class and racial orders permeate our ways of reading and relating to each other. Embarrassment and fear, however, have a silencing effect, eliding the extent to which young authors not only transcend but also creatively take up, inspect, and reshape such concepts as the "deprivation" that Lopate deplores.

It is possible to loosen the hold of embarrassment without letting go of critique. To acknowledge the limiting and sometimes destructive adult-made circumstances of youth writing does not betray young people but rather opens attention to the ways in which they understand, navigate, and leverage their authorial conditions. Children's writing practices under constraint may certainly sharpen readers' understandings of power and resistance. More than that, these texts open a view of how young people create for their own purposes, bending adult-shaped authorship to their own ends.

A fresh approach to youth authorship and an alternative to receptive pessimism emerges in the work of June Jordan, whose work first inspired this book. At the same conference that featured the Simon Gratz High School panel, Jordan gave a talk that drew on her experience with the Voice of the Children to propose a theory of children's poetry and, by extension, poetry in general. Later published in Larrick's book, Jordan's essay, "Children and the Hungering For," begins: "Let me tell you about poetry as something natural. Let me tell you how poetry, how the hungering for metaphors infinitely based on you and me, is more natural than everyday dialog. If you will believe me, maybe more of us can affirm the human purpose of poetry." The repeated appeal "Let me tell you" and the contingency of "if you will believe me" model Jordan's theory of interpersonal connection. Venturing far from any "normal aesthetic standards," Jordan proposes that the power of poetry arises from an interpersonal impulse that is rooted in infancy. From their first days of life, young people "embody *a hungering for*: Children fill their lives with learning: they hurtle themselves outward, into the greater reality, hoping to embrace, without perishing." The yearning, ever-reaching pull of human connection shapes the phrase *a hungering for*. With its unconventional dangling preposition, the phrase models a fresh relationship to language. Jordan's *hungering for* is an ethic, an affect, and an interpretive framework. In a rebuke to those critics who take children's voices as individualistic cries of authenticity, Jordan argues that "poetry is valid because it includes beyond the self."[39]

Jordan practiced this "inclu[sion] beyond the self" in part by carrying the imprint of her young literary collaborators into her broader career. The Voice of the Children's influence is clear in two works by Jordan that engage not only with poetics but specifically with the dynamics of reception: the 1969 book *Who Look at Me* and the early 1990s project Poetry for the People. *Who Look at Me*, Jordan's first published book, juxtaposes representations of Black people by both Black and white artists with a poetic text in which a young Black speaker thinks with, through, and beyond the images to meditate on a child's American life. This unusual picture book was created during Jordan's work with the Voice of the Children and is steeped in the voices and perspectives of 1960s–1970s young poets. The speaker of the book—who asks, "Is that how we look to you / a partial nothing clearly real?" and "WHO LOOK AT ME / WHO SEE?"—conducts a reception of reception akin to the questions of Juan's peer, as well as the work of the Voice of the Children poet Linda Curry, explored in chapter 1.[40] In *Who Look at Me*, as in the work of young writers of the time, this interrogation of reception functions not only to school readers but also to advance young speakers' self-studies: the confrontation of a mixed bag of portraits as a means of self-portraiture. In Kevin Quashie's framing of *Who Look at Me*, the "political work of the book is not centrally in confronting whiteness but more in displaying black engagedness, in its showcasing a speaker who is alert and alive."[41] *Who Look at Me* thus demonstrates Jordan's own receptivity, as she extended young poets' sensibilities and philosophies into her wide-ranging projects.

Decades later, Jordan brought key elements of her work with the Voice of the Children into her beloved and still-running project at the University of California, Berkeley: Poetry for the People. Founded in 1991, Poetry for the People grew out of Jordan's university poetry courses, which emphasized inclusive community within the classroom and insisted on poetic engagement outside the classroom, taking the creation of poems as a foundation for true community: a "fearless democratic society."[42] In Poetry for the People, as in the Voice of the Children, Jordan emphasized the public circulation and celebration of students' work. Jordan found it vital for Poetry for the People's students to experience "why public performance, publication, and media appearances are natural and necessary steps to the acquirement of power through language."[43] The rationale for this public life of poetry draws on her circa-1970 language of "hungering for." Jordan's essay on Poetry for the People explains: "Because poetry is the medium for telling the truth, and because a poem is antithetical to lies/evasions and superficiality, anyone who becomes a practicing poet has an excellent chance of becoming somebody real, somebody known, self-defined, and attuned to and listening and *hungering for* kindred real voices utterly/articulately different from his or her own voice."[44] Here, again, poetry starts with self-witness. To be "real" is first to tell the truth to and of oneself, to be "self-defined." It is through this interior receptivity that the poet may develop a broader practice of mutual reception. The poet reaches out in an act of "hungering for" those who are simultaneously "kindred," in that they are fellow truth-tellers, and "utterly/articulately different," capable of affecting each other and changing each other's minds. The reaching, questioning, hungering pull of 1960s–1970s young poets suffuses Jordan's approach to Poetry for the People. That very connection, moreover, illustrates Jordan's own "hungering" practice of learning with and from the young.

Across the decades of her career, Jordan's theory of "hungering for" poetics resonates with the youth writing examined in this book. The young authors discussed in the preceding chapters are invested in observing, testing, and reshaping interpersonal ties and dynamics, including their relationship with themselves. In Jordan's ethic, children's poetry—and by extension, all poetry—should be read relationally. Importantly, Jordan's 1969 essay leaves open the object of children's hungering, which simply directs "outward, into the greater reality, hoping to embrace, without perishing." Jordan's repeated withholding of the objects of prepositions and transitive verbs—hungering for *what?* to embrace *whom?* to include *what* beyond the self?—holds at bay the ways in which children are essentialized and instrumentalized for immediate political ends. Jordan invites readers into a state of open process, unfulfilled yearning, and interpersonal contingency: a promising state for reading the poetry of children.

The Long Walks of Youth Writing

> Walk on Water
> Walk on a Leaf
> Hardest of all is
> Walk in Grief
> —W. N., "Jail-Life Walk"

B y the mid-1970s, public fascination with Black and Puerto Rican young writers had dwindled. As June Jordan observed in 1979, "At the end of the 1960's, American mass media rolled the cameras away from black life and the quantity of print on the subject became too small to read."[1] This disinvestment, along with the critical undermining of youth writing described in chapter 4, left the phenomenon of circa-1970 child authorship virtually unacknowledged. Despite this neglect, child authors of the Black Arts era found ways to extend their influence into the twenty-first century. In 2016, while researching this book, I experienced a shock of recognition when theater artist Anna Deavere Smith performed a fragment from the late 1960s youth poet W. N., reproduced in the epigraph to this section, in her play *Notes from the Field*.[2] The reappearance of W. N.'s verse reveals how U. S. culture continues to register the impact circa-1970 youth writing, despite little recognition of this history. Child authors of the Black Arts era still shape the American conception of youth voice as an anti-racist force, even while imparting imaginative possibilities beyond the bounds of a white supremacist state.

An examination of the "school-to-prison pipeline," the racist system of using schools to police and ultimately incarcerate young people of color, *Notes from the Field* was produced in multiple cities before being filmed and released for streaming by HBO in 2018. In her signature style, Smith interviews diverse individuals, including teachers, activists, and a formerly incarcerated person who recalls his own school experiences, and then reembodies these individuals' words in solo performance. Smith historicizes these contemporary voices by performing a 1971 monologue from James Baldwin in *A Rap on Race*, his public conversation with Margaret Mead, in which he quotes one of the era's young poets.

> Luckily, I'm not fifteen, but if I were, how in the world would I find any respect for human life, or any sense of history? . . . I read a little book called *The Way It Spozed to Be*. And it was poetry and things written by little black children, Mexican, Puerto Rican children. . . . One boy wrote a poem. Sixteen years old, he was in prison. It ended, four lines I never will forget: "Walk on water, walk on a leaf, hardest of all / Is walk in grief." So what I'm trying to get at, I hope, is that there is tremendous national, global, moral waste. . . . What should we do about the children?[3]

An incarcerated sixteen-year-old poet's voice has traveled from a teacher's files into an anthology, then onto the stage with Baldwin and Mead, into the book version of *A Rap on Race*, and, decades later, into Smith's 2016 performance, 2018 HBO film, and 2019 book. Although Baldwin almost perfectly quotes these poetic lines from memory—only substituting "to walk on grief" for "walk in grief," an error that Smith corrects—he misnames the book from which he quotes. The poem, "Jail-Life Walk," actually appears in *The Me Nobody Knows* anthology, with an editor's note that sixteen-year-old W. N. "wrote this poem while awaiting sentencing at Youth House."[4] The same poem was also loosely adapted into a song in the 1970 musical adaptation of *The Me*. Reading W. N.'s "Jail-Life Walk" in its entirety reveals how the poem has drawn attention across half a century.

W. N.'s first stanza describes how incarceration disciplines movement: "Walk in the Day / Walk in the Night / Walk a chalk Line / Walk it right."[5] W. N. here draws on the expression "walking the chalk," or adhering to the rules of prison life under white racial domination (the color of chalk).[6] In the context of "Jail-Life Walk," W. N.'s chalk line conjures a young person being marched in and out of courts and inserted into systems that constrain bodily and behavioral mobility and demand impossible balancing acts. These systems enact a terrible suspension of time, as denoted by the poet's use of hypnotic repetition and sleepless insistence on both "Day" and "Night." This initial emphasis on obedience and pragmatic survival, however, breaks down in the following three stanzas.

The poet spins out varied and increasingly strange images of walking, concluding with the stanza quoted by Baldwin and Smith: "Walk on Water / Walk on a Leaf / Hardest of all is / Walk in Grief."[7] As the catalog of journeys unfolds, the verb *walk* reads less like an imperative—what one must do—and more like an abbreviated infinitive or imaginative supposition: What if one were to walk in this way? From the miracle of walking on water to the insect-like fineness of walking on a single leaf, the poem explores difficult and delicate acts of movement.

By addressing the concept of travel itself, "Jail-Life Walk" seems to anticipate its journey across space and time, crossing spheres of authorship and discourses about youth crises. Somewhat like the poetic speaker, the poem itself has passed through many sets of adult hands, outside of a young person's control. Through this process, poem and poet may be altered or misrepresented. For instance, in both Baldwin's commentary and *The Me* musical, W. N. is gendered male, even though Joseph's anthology does not indicate the poet's gender; both boys and girls were incarcerated at Youth House. We cannot know, moreover, how the work may have been edited or mistyped by adults. Despite the risk of misrepresentation, W. N.'s original work is equipped to endure and to comment on its own travels. "Jail-Life Walk" demonstrates the robustness of circa-1970 youth writing, which contains built-in rhetorical mechanisms for highlighting and theorizing the terms of its own production and reception.

W. N.'s words are particularly important within *Notes from the Field* because despite the show's concern for youth, the youngest interlocutors that Smith dramatizes are two eighteen-year-old activists, Allen Bullock and Niya Kenny. Kenny made national news when she took cellphone footage of a peer being violently assaulted by a school police officer and was then arrested herself for speaking out in the classroom against the assault. In *Notes from the Field*, Kenny's youthful voice is interwoven with an older journalist who narrates much of her story, leaving the narrative of the play leaning heavily toward adult perspectives. Smith's citing of W. N. via Baldwin follows this pattern of adult-mediated youth voice.

Within a largely adult chorus of voices, W. N.'s words open a brief but vivid moment of youth perspective in *Notes from the Field* that also demonstrates the 1960s–1970s historical roots of Kenny's position. W. N.'s poetic buildup to the incomparable journey of a "Walk in Grief" portrays youth incarceration as steeped in loss and heartbreak. Rather than providing a straightforward testimony of suffering, however, W. N. suggests a double itinerary, contrasting the physical or external marches that the poet must perform with a private, interior experience. Whatever chalk line or pipeline feet must follow, the writer is poetically walking in another direction, in which "grief" swerves from the straight and narrow. This is the inner life of youth that Baldwin invokes: that which, he warns, is being put to "tremendous . . . waste."

As W. N.'s poetic cameo demonstrates, circa-1970 children's writing remains deeply embedded in US reckonings with racism. Young writers of the late 1960s and early 1970s imaginatively examined the era's rapidly innovating forms of racism, presciently documenting both a moment of radical promise and new forms of foreclosure and threat. These writers examined not only what it felt like to grow up amid such forces but also what it felt like to experience a post–civil rights racist regime while simultaneously being celebrated as the voices of ultimate truth. The young people of that time precisely described some of the same patterns of liberal and neoliberal power that scholars have reckoned with over the subsequent decades, such as the pitfalls of visibility politics. Circa-1970 youth writing indicates the value of keenly listening to young people of color as they observe the next generation's gathering storms. W. N. and peers, moreover, advance a conception of youth voice that surpasses the testimony of trauma. The mystic valence of "Jail-Life Walk," along with the dreamy, strange, and self-conscious twists of other circa-1970 youth writings, denote a level of young people's experience that is both expressive of and incompletely determined by the conditions of white supremacy.

In the face of circa-1970 young writers' creative work, Baldwin's despair for the "tremendous waste" of youth feels like an inadequate conclusion to his discussion of children's writing. Certainly, there is tremendous waste, and we cannot stand for the widespread neglect and disrespect of children. But there is also tremendous creative, intellectual, and political productivity among children, according to their own interests and ends. To Baldwin's question "What should we do about the children?" we may also ask: What do young people *themselves* want to do about the children? And what creative tactics have young people *already* developed to inspect, alter, or make the most of their position?

As I write, cries to "listen to the children" abound. The 1960s–1970s wave of attention to child authorship seeded today's proliferation of youth writing programs and publications, from the national nonprofit 826, which publishes frequent collections of student work and promises to "Write the Future," to national and local Youth Poet Laureate programs, which aim to "identify and celebrate exceptional youth poets who use their voice to inspire change," most famously Amanda Gorman.[8] These programs espouse a view that has become commonplace: that, in the words of the 826 program, "the power of young voices," particularly the voices of children of color, can enact social change, and that youth writing can lead to "a more just world." While visions of change-making children predate the 1960s, the yoking of child writers and social change—the belief that children can and should speak for justice movements—is deeply rooted in 1960s–1970s US culture. This belief, I argue, has been actively explored and reshaped by Black and Puerto Rican young people.

Today's young poets are asked both to galvanize the public and to inspire the next generation of children to do the same. Gorman herself recently demonstrated the potency of this process in her response to the recent surge in censorship of children's reading materials. In the spring of 2023, Gorman's "The Hill We Climb," written for Joseph Biden's presidential inauguration, was restricted from elementary-grade students at a Florida school after a parent accused the text of intending to "cause confusion and indoctrinate students."[9] The parent's complaint assumes a low-agency model of children's literacy, in which young people are vulnerable to being acted on. Gorman's public response to the banning, in contrast, emphasizes children's own literary output: "I've received countless letters and videos from children inspired by The Hill We Climb to write their own poems. Robbing children of the chance to find their voices in literature is a violation of their right to free thought and free speech."[10] Pointing to children's composition of letters, videos, and poems and portraying young people as active readers—participants in the task of "find[ing] their voices in literature"—Gorman recruits young authors to the battle against book banning. Given recent book bans' disproportionate targeting of texts written "by and about people of color and LGBTQ+ individuals," as PEN America documents and Gorman emphasizes, Gorman's response reveals how the figure of youth voice continues to loom large in anti-racist and social justice work.[11]

In the 2020s, as in the 1960s, the adulation of young writers has often failed to translate into material protection for vulnerable children. US liberalism treats children's voices, particularly those of non-white children, as the essence of voice itself: that which makes us better by its very airing, as if listening were the ultimate practice of justice. Yet the young people who publicly advocate for gun control, migrant justice, climate action, and the end of police violence might commiserate with the question of Juan's peer in chapter 4: "Could they really hear?" US public culture has a way of muffling children's voices in the very gesture of amplifying them—a pattern that young people themselves have long observed.

I am no longer convinced that we can get much done by admonishing each other to "listen to the children." Let us attend to children's words, not by moral imperative or political piety but because they are elegant, canny, funny, hypnotic, and packed with lessons about what it means to live and speak in an unequal America. When we trust children's understanding of their own authorial position, then we can perceive how they have already been making their mark on us, writing themselves into the heart of US culture.

Notes

INTRODUCTION

1 Elisa, untitled essay, in Caroline Mirthes and the Children of PS 15, *Can't You Hear Me Talking to You?* (New York: Bantam Books, 1971), 62. The young writers in this volume were assigned pseudonyms.

2 Elaine Avidon, Zoom conversation with author, February 22, 2024.

3 Sophie McCall, *First Person Plural: Aboriginal Storytelling and the Ethics of Collaborative Authorship* (Vancouver, BC: University of British Columbia Press, 2011), 4–5. Christine R. Cavalier, "Jane Johnston Schoolcraft's Sentimental Lessons: Native Literary Collaboration and Resistance," *MELUS: Multi-Ethnic Literature of the United States* 38, no. 1 (March 2013): 99.

4 Karen Sánchez-Eppler, *Dependent States: The Child's Part in Nineteenth-Century American Culture* (Chicago: University of Chicago Press, 2005), xxv.

5 Henry Louis Gates, *The Trials of Phillis Wheatley: America's First Black Poet and Her Encounters with the Founding Fathers* (New York: Civitas Books, 2003), 5–30. On Black Arts–era condemnations of Wheatley and later reckonings with her, see Gates, *Trials*, 78–80.

6 Howard Rambsy, *The Black Arts Enterprise and the Production of African American Poetry* (Ann Arbor: University of Michigan Press, 2013), 10.

7 June Jordan, "The Difficult Miracle of Black Poetry in America, or Something like a Sonnet for Phillis Wheatley," *Massachusetts Review* 27, no. 2 (Summer 1986): 252–62.

8 Robin D. G. Kelley, *Yo' Mama's Disfunktional! Fighting the Culture Wars in Urban America* (Boston: Beacon Press, 1997), 20.

9 Paula C. Austin, *Coming of Age in Jim Crow DC: Navigating the Politics of Everyday Life* (New York: New York University Press, 2019), 1. See also Crystal Lynn Webster, *Beyond the Boundaries of Childhood: African American Children in the Antebellum North* (Chapel Hill: University of North Carolina Press, 2021); LaKisha Michelle Simmons, *Crescent City Girls: The Lives of Young Black Women in Segregated New Orleans*, Gender & American Culture (Chapel Hill: University of North Carolina Press, 2015); Marcia Chatelain, *South Side Girls: Growing Up in the Great Migration* (Durham, NC: Duke University Press, 2015); Robin Bernstein, *Racial Innocence: Performing American Childhood from Slavery to Civil Rights* (New York: New York University Press, 2011); Mary Niall Mitchell,

Raising Freedom's Child: Black Children and Visions of the Future after Slavery (New York: New York University Press, 2008); Anna Mae Duane and Thomas Thurston, "Performing Freedom at the New York African Free School," in *Hope Is the First Great Blessing: Leaves from the African Free School Presentation Book, 1812–1826,* ed. David W. Blight et al. (New York: New York Historical Society, 2008), 17–25.

10 bell hooks, "Theory as Liberatory Practice," *Yale Journal of Law and Feminism* 4 (1991): 2.

11 Kevin Quashie, *Black Aliveness, or A Poetics of Being* (Durham, NC: Duke University Press, 2021); Kevin Quashie, *The Sovereignty of Quiet: Beyond Resistance in Black Culture* (New Brunswick, NJ: Rutgers University Press, 2012).

12 James Edward Smethurst, *The Black Arts Movement: Literary Nationalism in the 1960s and 1970s* (Chapel Hill: University of North Carolina Press, 2005), 101.

13 Smethurst, *Black Arts Movement,* 172–78. On the multicultural character of Black Arts and specifically the role of Puerto Rican writers and forms of Afro-Latinidad in the movement, see Michelle Joan Wilkinson, "'To Make a Poet Black': Canonizing Puerto Rican Poets in the Black Arts Movement," in *New Thoughts on the Black Arts Movement,* ed. Lisa Gail Collins and Margo Natalie Crawford (New Brunswick, NJ: Rutgers University Press, 2006), 317–32; Rod Hernandez, "Latin Soul: Cross-Cultural Connections between the Black Arts Movement and Pocho-Che," in Collins and Crawford, *New Thoughts,* 333–48. Certainly, young writers did not work exclusively within the terms of Black Arts; they also worked within distinct Puerto Rican and developing Nuyorican literary and cultural currents of the time.

14 Rambsy, *Black Arts Enterprise,* vii.

15 Smethurst, *Black Arts Movement,* 122.

16 "Note to the first paperback edition of *Black Fire,*" reprinted in Amiri Baraka and Larry Neal, *Black Fire: An Anthology of Afro-American Writing,* rev. ed. (Baltimore, MD: Black Classic Press, 2007), n.p.; Ed Bullins, "MALCOLM: '71, or Publishing Blackness (Based upon a Real Experience)," *Black Scholar* 6, no. 9 (June 1975): 85; Addison Gayle, ed., *The Black Aesthetic* (Garden City, NY: Doubleday, 1971), xxi. On Bullins's play, see Mike Sell, *Avant-Garde Performance and the Limits of Criticism: Approaching the Living Theatre, Happenings/Fluxus, and the Black Arts Movement* (Ann Arbor: University of Michigan Press, 2005), 218–20.

17 Margo Natalie Crawford, *Black Post-Blackness: The Black Arts Movement and Twenty-First-Century Aesthetics* (Champaign: University of Illinois Press, 2017), 36, 3. See also GerShun Avilez, *Radical Aesthetics and Modern Black Nationalism* (Champaign: University of Illinois Press, 2016).

18 Katharine Capshaw, *Civil Rights Childhood: Picturing Liberation in African American Photobooks* (Minneapolis: University of Minnesota Press, 2014), 155, 157.

19 David Grundy, *A Black Arts Poetry Machine: Amiri Baraka and the Umbra Poets* (New York: Bloomsbury, 2019), 4.

20 For recent literary scholarship examining young people's agency as readers, fans, authors, performers, and collaborators, see Victoria Ford Smith, *Between Generations: Collaborative Authorship in the Golden Age of Children's Literature* (Jackson: University Press of Mississippi, 2017); Richard Flynn, "Introduction: Disputing the Role of Agency in Children's Literature and Culture," *Jeunesse* 8, no. 1 (Summer 2016): 248–53; Marah Gubar, "Risky Business: Talking about Children in Children's Literature Criticism," *Children's Literature Association Quarterly* 38, no. 4 (Winter 2013): 450–57; Karen Sánchez-Eppler, "Marks of Possession: Methods for an Impossible Subject," *PMLA* 126, no. 1 (January

2011): 151–59; Karen Sánchez-Eppler, "In the Archives of Childhood," in *The Children's Table: Childhood Studies and the Humanities* (Athens: University of Georgia Press, 2013), 213–37; Jennifer Coletta Tullos, "'We Gon' Fight, Emmett': Performing Childhood and Innocence as Resistance in Black Youth Slam Poetry," *The Lion and the Unicorn* 43, no. 2 (April 2019): 261–81.

21 Rachel Conrad, "'We Are Masters at Childhood': Time and Agency in Poetry by, for, and about Children," *Jeunesse* 5, no. 2 (Winter 2013): 124–50.

22 Marilisa Jiménez García, *Side by Side: US Empire, Puerto Rico, and the Roots of American Youth Literature and Culture* (Jackson: University Press of Mississippi, 2021), 7.

23 Jiménez García, *Side by Side*; Conrad, "We Are Masters at Childhood"; Rachel Conrad, *Time for Childhoods: Young Poets and Questions of Agency* (Amherst: University of Massachusetts Press, 2020); Capshaw, *Civil Rights Childhood*; Nazera Sadiq Wright, *Black Girlhood in the Nineteenth Century* (Urbana: University of Illinois Press, 2016); Richard Flynn, "'Affirmative Acts': Language, Childhood, and Power in June Jordan's Cross-Writing," *Children's Literature* 30 (2002): 159–85; Michelle Martin, *Brown Gold: Milestones of African American Children's Picture Books, 1845–2002* (New York: Routledge, 2004).

24 Conrad, *Time for Childhoods*, xii.

25 Katharine Capshaw Smith, "The Brownies' Book and the Roots of African American Children's Literature," *The Tar Baby and the Tomahawk: Race and Ethnic Images in American Children's Literature, 1880–1939*, http://childlit.unl.edu/topics/edi.harlem.html.

26 Student Nonviolent Coordinating Committee, *Freedom School Poetry*, ed. Nancy Cooper (Atlanta, GA: Student Nonviolent Coordinating Committee, 1965). I thank Katharine Capshaw for introducing this text to me.

27 James Baldwin, *Little Man, Little Man*, illustrated by Yoran Cazac (New York: Dial Press, 1976); Virginia Hamilton, *The Planet of Junior Brown* (New York: Macmillan, 1971).

28 June Jordan, *Who Look at Me* (New York: Thomas Y. Crowell, 1969); June Jordan, *His Own Where* (New York: Crowell, 1971); Amy Fish, "Dreaming 'for Real': June Jordan's *His Own Where* as Youth History," *Lion and the Unicorn* 43, no. 2 (April 2019): 196–214.

29 Nancy Larrick, "The All-White World of Children's Books," *Saturday Review*, September 11, 1965, 63.

30 See, for example, Nancy Larrick, *I Heard a Scream in the Street* (New York: M. Evans, 1970); Nancy Larrick and Eve Merriam, eds., *Male and Female Under 18: Frank Comments from Young People about Their Sex Roles Today* (New York: Discus Books, 1973); Nancy Larrick, ed., *Somebody Turned on a Tap in These Kids: Poetry and Young People Today* (New York: Delacorte Press, 1971).

31 Clive Barnes, "Off Broadway Musical Makes Shift to the Helen Hayes a Triumph," *New York Times*, January 1, 1971.

32 Luis, "A Wish (A Real One)," in Mirthes and the Children of PS 15, *Can't You Hear Me Talking to You?*, 106.

33 On the "shift from beloved, all-black schools to white schools where black students were always seen as interlopers, as not really belonging," see bell hooks, introduction to *Teaching to Transgress* (New York: Routledge, 1994), 3.

34 Phillip Lopate, *Being with Children: A High-Spirited Personal Account of Teaching Writing, Theater, and Videotape* (New York: New Press, 2008), 11.

35 Sonia Nieto, "Puerto Rican Students in U.S. Schools: A Brief History," in *Puerto Rican Students in U.S. Schools*, ed. Sonia Nieto (Mahwah, NJ: Routledge, 2000), 18; Melissa

Rivera and Pedro Pedraza, "The Spirit of Transformation: An Education Reform Move-ment in a New York City Latino/a Community," in Nieto, *Puerto Rican Students*, 223–43.

36 On Head Start, see "Head Start History," Office of Head Start, Administration for Chil-dren & Families, 2023, https://www.acf.hhs.gov/ohs/about/history-head-start; as well as Capshaw's work on the Head Start preschool program run by the Child Development Group of Mississippi, in *Civil Rights Childhood*, 121–53.

37 Jacob S. Dorman, "Dreams Defended and Deferred: The Brooklyn Schools Crisis of 1968 and Black Power's Influence on Rabbi Meir Kahane," *American Jewish History* 100, no. 3 (2016): 411–37; Fred Ferretti, "New York's Black Anti-Semitism Scare," *Columbia Journal-ism Review* 8, no. 3 (Fall 1969): 18–28.

38 Julius Lester, *Lovesong: Becoming a Jew* (New York: Henry Holt, 1988), 50–51.

39 Avidon, Zoom conversation with author.

40 Russell John Rickford, *We Are an African People: Independent Education, Black Power, and the Radical Imagination* (New York: Oxford University Press, 2016).

41 Xaé Alicia Reyes, "Return Migrant Students: Yankee Go Home?," in Nieto, *Puerto Rican Students*, 39–67; Jesse Hoffnung-Garskof, *A Tale of Two Cities: Santo Domingo and New York after 1950* (Princeton, NJ: Princeton University Press, 2008), 132–62; Rickford, *We Are an African People*, 47–48.

42 Paul Montgomery, "Lane High School Consolidating Sessions to Tighten Security," *New York Times*, November 4, 1969.

43 Smethurst, *Black Arts Movement*, 14.

44 James R. Squire et al., "The National Interest and the Teaching of English: A Report on the Status of the Profession" (Champaign, IL: National Council of Teachers of English, 1961); Joseph Harris, "After Dartmouth: Growth and Conflict in English," *College English* 53, no. 6 (October 1991): 631.

45 Rebecca Onion, *Innocent Experiments: Childhood and the Culture of Popular Science in the United States* (Chapel Hill: University of North Carolina Press, 2016), 88.

46 Alice Glarden Brand, "Creative Writing in English Education: An Historical Perspec-tive," *Journal of Education* 162, no. 4 (Fall 1980): 65–69.

47 See, for example, Jonathan Kozol, *Death at an Early Age* (Boston, MA: Houghton Mifflin, 1967); Herbert R. Kohl, *36 Children* (New York: New American Library, 1967); Andrew Summers, ed., *Me the Flunkie: Yearbook of a School for Failures* (Greenwich, CT: Fawcett, 1970).

48 Irving Benig, ed., *The Children: Poems and Prose from Bedford-Stuyvesant* (New York: Grove Press, 1971), vii.

49 Phillip Lopate, "Issues of Language," in *Journal of a Living Experiment: A Documentary History of the First Ten Years of Teachers and Writers Collaborative*, ed. Phillip Lopate (New York: Teachers and Writers Collaborative, 1979), 100.

50 Evie Shockley, "The Black Arts Movement and Black Aesthetics," in *The Cambridge Companion to Modern American Poetry*, ed. Walter Kalaidjian (New York: Cambridge University Press, 2015), 183.

51 On young poets' verb tense shifts, see Conrad, *Time for Childhoods*, 96, 104.

52 On Black English, ranging from the moment of circa-1970 youth writing to the present day, see June Jordan, "White English/Black English: The Politics of Translation (1972)," in *Civil Wars* (New York: Touchstone, 1995), 59–73; June Jordan, "Nobody Mean More to Me Than You and the Future Life of Willie Jordan," *Harvard Educational Review* 58, no. 3 (September 1988): 363–75; April Baker-Bell, *Linguistic Justice: Black Language, Literacy,*

Identity, and Pedagogy (New York: Routledge, 2020). While I use the circa-1970 term *Black English*, I borrow the term *White Mainstream English* from Baker-Bell's contemporary work in youth linguistics and literacy.

53 Rambsy, *Black Arts Enterprise*, 49–70; Baraka and Neal, *Black Fire*; Miguel Algarín and Miguel Piñero, *A Nuyorican Poetry: An Anthology of Puerto Rican Words and Feelings* (New York: Morrow, 1975).

54 Paul Saint-Amour, "Weak Theory, Weak Modernism," *Modernism/Modernity* 3, no. 3 (August 2018), https://modernismmodernity.org/articles/weak-theory-weak-modernism.

55 For an example of such a concentrated study, see Grundy, *Black Arts Poetry Machine*. See also the argument for extended close readings of individual poets, particularly those with marginalized identities, in Grundy, *Black Arts Poetry Machine*, 7.

56 Daniel Kane, *All Poets Welcome: The Lower East Side Poetry Scene in the 1960s* (Berkeley: University of California Press, 2003), 129, 124.

57 On Jordan and Major's reading that evening, see Aleksandar Nejgebauer, "America the Poetical, and Otherwise," *New Republic* 160, no. 17 (April 26, 1969): 20. On the children's experience of April 4, as recollected by Terri Bush, see Conrad, *Time for Childhoods*, 127. Goode's poem appeared in a column by Nat Hentoff, "Shot with a Hot Rot Grin," *Village Voice*, April 11, 1968.

58 Sister Francis Mary to June Jordan and Terri Bush, January 22, 1970, Voice of the Children collection of Terri Bush, box 1, Schlesinger Library, Harvard University.

59 Lorenzo Thomas, "Alea's Children: The Avant-Garde on the Lower East Side, 1960–1970," *African American Review* 27, no. 4 (1993): 573.

60 On Levertov, see Miguel Ortiz, "Latin Nostalgia," in Lopate, *Journal of a Living Experiment*, 295.

61 Marvin Hoffman, "Two and a Half Years," in Lopate, *Journal of a Living Experiment*, 263.

62 "Poetry, Song Sessions Set," *New York Amsterdam News*, May 1, 1971; Phyl Garland, "The Gifted Child: Kali and Chandra," *Ebony*, August 1974, 97. Both sources cited in Capshaw, *Civil Rights Childhood*, 169.

63 Garland, "Gifted Child," 96.

64 I refer to Alvin Curry by first name to distinguish him from his sister Linda Curry, a central figure in chapter 1.

65 In its first decade, T&W included the writers "Herbert Kohl, Muriel Rukeyser, Anne Sexton, Kenneth Koch, Grace Paley, David Henderson, Benjamin DeMott, June Jordan, Nat Hentoff, Victor Hernández Cruz, Joel Oppenheimer, Ron Padgett, Florence Howe, Mark Mirsky, John Holt, Jay Wright, Rosellen Brown, Sonia Sanchez, Louise Gluck, Felipe Luciano, Pedro Pietri, David Shapiro, A. B. Spellman, Tom Weatherly, Wesley Brown, Maria Irene Fornés, Robert Silvers, Jonathan Baumbach, Bill Berkson, Armand Schwerner, Sidney Goldfarb, Calvin Trillin, Richard Elrnan, Leonard Jenkin, Dick Gallup, Meredith Sue Willis, Lennox Raphael, Karen Hubert, Richard Perry, and Bill Zavatsky, to name only the most widely-published." Lopate, introduction to *Journal of a Living Experiment*, 7.

66 Karen Kennerly, interview by Lopate, in Lopate, *Journal of a Living Experiment*, 86–89.

67 Herbert Kohl, interview by Lopate, in Lopate, *Journal of a Living Experiment*, 34.

68 Robert Jackson, "Alvin Curry: 'The Man of Many Fables,'" cover illustration, *Teachers and Writers Collaborative Newsletter* 1, no. 1 (September 1967), Teachers & Writers Collaborative organizational archives, New York.

69 Smethurst, *Black Arts Movement*, 138.

70 Thomas, "Alea's Children," 573.

71 For an argument against age in bylines, see Conrad, *Time for Childhoods*, 23, 112.

72 John F. Kennedy, "Remarks upon Signing the Juvenile Delinquency and Youth Offenses Control Act" (Washington, D.C., September 22, 1961); Elizabeth Hinton, *From the War on Poverty to the War on Crime: The Making of Mass Incarceration in America* (Cambridge, MA: Harvard University Press, 2016), 2–3.

73 See, for example, Amir A. Gilmore and Pamela J. Bettis, "Antiblackness and the Adultification of Black Children in a U.S. Prison Nation," in *Oxford Research Encyclopedia of Education*, March 25, 2021, https://doi.org/10.1093/acrefore/9780190264093.013.1293; Laila Hlass, "The Adultification of Immigrant Children," *Georgetown Immigration Law Journal* 34, no. 2 (Winter 2020): 199–263.

74 See the anti-racist and decolonial theorization of the term *youth literature and culture* in Jiménez García, *Side by Side*, 6–7.

75 See, for example, Thomas Crisp et al., "The Complexities of #OwnVoices in Children's Literature," *Journal of Children's Literature* 46, no. 2 (Fall 2020): 5–7.

76 Tiya Miles, *All That She Carried: The Journey of Ashley's Sack, a Black Family Keepsake* (New York: Random House, 2021), 288.

CHAPTER 1

1 Phillip Solomon, untitled ["black child"], in June Jordan and Terri Bush, eds., *The Voice of the Children* (New York: Holt, Rinehart and Winston, 1970), 51; LeRoi Jones, *The System of Dante's Hell* (New York: Grove, 1965), 153.

2 Thomas A. Johnson, "Renaissance in Black Poetry Expresses an Anger," *New York Times*, April 25, 1969.

3 Rachel Conrad, *Time for Childhoods: Young Poets and Questions of Agency* (Amherst: University of Massachusetts Press, 2020), 141. See also Richard Flynn's account of Jordan's broader project of work for children, in Richard Flynn, "'Affirmative Acts': Language, Childhood, and Power in June Jordan's Cross-Writing," *Children's Literature* 30 (2002): 159–85.

4 Phillip Brian Harper, "Nationalism and Social Division in Black Arts Poetry of the 1960s," *Critical Inquiry* 19, no. 2 (Winter 1993): 248.

5 Harper, "Nationalism and Social Division," 247.

6 Kevin Quashie, *Black Aliveness, or A Poetics of Being* (Durham, NC: Duke University Press, 2021), 7.

7 Quashie, *Black Aliveness*, 28.

8 Kenneth Koch, interview by Phillip Lopate, in *Journal of a Living Experiment: A Documentary History of the First Ten Years of Teachers and Writers Collaborative*, ed. Phillip Lopate (New York: Teachers and Writers Collaborative, 1979), 274.

9 June Meyer, "You Can't See the Trees for the School," *Urban Review* 2, no. 3 (December 1967): 14. Parentheticals within this source represent June (Meyer) Jordan's own narrative insertion into Cruz's words. Though at the time using her married name, June Meyer, she would soon return to using her original name, June Jordan. I refer to her as June Jordan throughout for the sake of clarity.

10 Stefano Harney and Fred Moten, "The University and the Undercommons: Seven Theses," *Social Text* 22, no. 2 (Summer 2004): 101–15.

11 Herbert Kohl, interview by Lopate in Lopate, *Journal of a Living Experiment*, 27.

12 Kohl, in Lopate, *Journal of a Living Experiment*, 37.

13 Although Cruz seems to have joined the Saturday workshop with Jordan only for the first few weeks, he remained involved with T&W long-term. Records suggest that the Curry family moved from Harlem to Brooklyn between the time of Alvin's sixth-grade class with Kohl and the formation of the Voice of the Children.

14 Mary Kelley, "'Talents Committed to Your Care': Reading and Writing Radical Abolitionism in Antebellum America," *New England Quarterly* 88, no. 1 (February 2015): 71, 39.

15 June Jordan, "'The Voice of the Children' Diaries," in Lopate, *Journal of a Living Experiment*, 138. I corroborate this printing of Jordan's diaries with the documents available in her papers at Schlesinger Library. T&W does not possess copies of 1960s–1970s members' workshop diaries.

16 Jordan, "'The Voice of the Children' Diaries," in Lopate, *Journal of a Living Experiment*, 143.

17 bell hooks, "Homeplace: A Site of Resistance," *Yearning: Race, Gender, and Cultural Politics* (Boston: South End Press, 1990), 41–42.

18 Jordan, "'The Voice of the Children' Diaries," in Lopate, *Journal of a Living Experiment*, 147–49; "Child Writers of Bed-Stuy Publish a Book," December 19, 1970, unattributed news clipping, June Jordan Papers, box 54, Schlesinger Library, Harvard University.

19 bell hooks, introduction to *Teaching to Transgress* (New York: Routledge, 1994), 7.

20 Vanessa Howard, *A Screaming Whisper: Poems* (New York: Holt, Rinehart and Winston, 1972). See analysis of Howard's work in Conrad, *Time for Childhoods*.

21 Quashie, *Black Aliveness*, 95, 37.

22 Linda Curry, untitled ["fear have I"], in Jordan and Bush, *Voice of the Children*, 40.

23 Curry, untitled ["fear have I"], in Jordan and Bush, *Voice of the Children*, 40.

24 Sun Ra and his Myth Science Arkestra, *We Travel the Spaceways* (Chicago: Saturn, 1967).

25 Jodi Melamed, *Represent and Destroy: Rationalizing Violence in the New Racial Capitalism* (Minneapolis: University of Minnesota Press, 2011), 51.

26 Margo Natalie Crawford, *Black Post-Blackness: The Black Arts Movement and Twenty-First-Century Aesthetics* (Champaign: University of Illinois Press, 2017), 33; italics in original.

27 "Linda X" [Curry], untitled ["When you burn you earn your"], quoted in Jordan, untitled partial typescript draft on the Voice of the Children, n.d. [March–April 1969?], June Jordan Papers, box 63. This poem was likely written in the spring of 1969. On the circumstances of Curry's writing, see June Jordan to Gayl [Jones?], "Telegram Sent Black Womanhood Weekend, Conn. College," April 17, 1969, June Jordan Papers, box 21; Gayl [Jones?] to Jordan, April 21, 1969, June Jordan Papers, box 86.

28 I borrow terminology and linguistic analysis here from April Baker-Bell, *Linguistic Justice: Black Language, Literacy, Identity, and Pedagogy* (New York: Routledge, 2020).

29 June Jordan, "White English/Black English: The Politics of Translation," reprinted in June Jordan, *Civil Wars* (New York: Touchstone, 1995), 73.

30 LeRoi Jones and Larry Neal, eds., *Black Fire: An Anthology of Afro-American Writing* (New York: Morrow, 1968), 224.

31 Linda Curry, "For Nina Simone wherever you are," in Jordan and Bush, *Voice of the Children*, 46.

32 Daphne A. Brooks, "Nina Simone's Triple Play," *Callaloo* 34, no. 1 (Winter 2011): 180, 177.

33 W. E. B. Du Bois, *The Souls of Black Folk: Essays and Sketches* (Chicago: A. C. McClurg, 1903; Project Gutenberg, 2021), https://www.gutenberg.org/files/408/408-h/408-h.htm.

34 On Jordan and Major's reading that evening, see Aleksandar Nejgebauer, "America the Poetical, and Otherwise," *New Republic* 160, no. 17 (April 26, 1969): 20. On the children's experience of April 4, as recollected by Terri Bush, see Conrad, *Time for Childhoods*, 127.

35 Regarding reprintings of "April 4 1968," the poem appears in Virginia Olsen Baron, ed., *Here I Am! An Anthology of Poems Written by Young People in Some of America's Minority Groups* (New York: E. P. Dutton, 1969), 48–49. Goode also reported in 1970, "I was published in the Village Voice, (April 4th 1968) Columbia Teachers Manual, (I am waiting) and in the future I would be published in New Voices [or *Now Voices*]." Michael Goode, biographical statement submission for *Soulscript*, June Jordan Papers, box 53.

36 Michael Goode, "April 4 1968," in Jordan and Bush, *Voice of the Children*, 56.

37 Goode, "April 4 1968," in Jordan and Bush, *Voice of the Children*, 56–57.

38 Goode, "April 4 1968," in Jordan and Bush, *Voice of the Children*, 57.

39 Peter B. Levy, *The Great Uprising: Race Riots in Urban America during the 1960s* (Cambridge, UK: Cambridge University Press, 2018), 153.

40 *"Dear Dr. King . . ." A Tribute in Words and Pictures* (Jamaica, NY: Buckingham Enterprises, 1968); Public Schools of the District of Columbia, Model School Division, *Children of Cardozo Tell It Like It Is* (Cambridge, MA: Education Development Center, 1968).

41 "Child Writers of Bed-Stuy."

42 Michael Goode, "April 4 1968," and Zelda Wirtshafter, director's note, in *Teachers and Writers Collaborative Newsletter* 1, no. 3 (1968): n.p.

43 Nat Hentoff, "Shot with a Hot Rot Grin," *Village Voice*, April 11, 1968. According to Bush's correspondence, Goode was pleased with Hentoff's coverage and sought to meet him. Terri Bush to Nat Hentoff, August 7, 1969, Voice of the Children collection of Terri Bush, box 1, Schlesinger Library, Harvard University.

44 Lopate, *Journal of a Living Experiment*, 106.

45 Katharine Capshaw, *Civil Rights Childhood: Picturing Liberation in African American Photobooks* (Minneapolis: University of Minnesota Press, 2014), 172.

46 Lopate, *Journal of a Living Experiment*, 106.

47 Stokely Carmichael, "What We Want," *New York Review of Books* 7 (Sep. 22, 1966): 5.

48 On the workshop's correction policy, see Jordan, untitled partial typescript draft on the Voice of the Children, n.d. [March–April 1969?], June Jordan Papers, box 63; Lopate, *Journal of a Living Experiment*, 151; Marvin Hoffman, "The Other Mouth: Writing in the Schools," *Childhood Education* 47, no. 2 (November 1970): 79–83.

49 June Jordan, afterword to Jordan and Bush, *Voice of the Children*, 96.

50 Christopher Meyer, "Wonderful New York," in Jordan and Bush, *Voice of the Children*, 11. © Christopher D. Meyer, 1970.

51 Terri Bush to president of Volkswagen of America, June 24, 1969; June Meyer Jordan to Herbert M. Samuel, May 24, 1969, Voice of the Children collection of Terri Bush, box 1.

52 On the group's demise, see CNS, "Children's Voices Stilled," *Amsterdam News*, November 13, 1971.

53 Many of Winand's photos, as well as her reminiscences of the group, are preserved in the Papers of Anna Winand, Schlesinger Library, Harvard University.

54 Ellen Jaffe, "June Jordan and the Language of Your Life," *Against the Current* 100 (September/October 2002).

55 June Jordan to "Visitors and Adult Friends of the Children," 1969–70, June Jordan Papers, Box 54. The document header lists both Jordan and Bush but the letter is signed solely by Jordan. © Christopher D. Meyer, 1970.

56 June Jordan to Zelda Wirtshafter, February 12, 1968, in Lopate, *Journal of a Living Experiment*, 146. © Christopher D. Meyer, 1979. I have not found Wirtshafter's letters to Jordan. On the letter to Wirtshafter in the context of Jordan's larger project of work for children, see Flynn, 163–65.

57 Melamed, 14.

58 Stephen M. Joseph, ed., *The Me Nobody Knows: Children's Voices from the Ghetto* (New York: Avon Books, 1969); Ana Ohenewaa, ed., *I Am Somebody! Stories and Poems by Black Children* (Boston: Ginn, 1970); Nicholas Anthony Duva, ed., *Somebody Real: Voices of City Children* (Rockaway, NJ: American Faculty Press, 1972); Virginia Olsen Baron, ed., *Here I Am! An Anthology of Poems Written by Young People in Some of America's Minority Groups* (New York: E. P. Dutton, 1969).

CHAPTER 2

1 Carmen, "You've Got to Fight the Right Way," in Caroline Mirthes and the Children of PS 15, *Can't You Hear Me Talking to You?* (New York: Bantam Books, 1971), 88.

2 Young Lords Party, "13 Point Program and Platform," October 1969. Reprinted by Latino/a Education Network Service, http://palante.org/13%20Pt%20Program-1st.htm.

3 "Children's Voices of Hope and Despair," *New York Times*, April 9, 1971.

4 Mirthes, *Can't You Hear Me?*, 140–42.

5 For a markedly different view of the Lower East Side in the era, see, for instance, Urayoan Noel, *In Visible Movement: Nuyorican Poetry from the Sixties to Slam* (Iowa City: University of Iowa Press, 2014); Daniel Kane, *All Poets Welcome: The Lower East Side Poetry Scene in the 1960s* (Berkeley: University of California Press, 2003).

6 "Children's Voices."

7 Elizabeth Hinton, *From the War on Poverty to the War on Crime: The Making of Mass Incarceration in America* (Boston: Harvard University Press, 2016), 122–23.

8 Michael Sasha King, "The Right to Tell: Listening Practices, Race, and Recordings, 1947–1974," PhD dissertation, Harvard University, 2020.

9 Rachel Conrad, *Time for Childhoods: Young Poets and Questions of Agency* (Amherst: University of Massachusetts Press, 2020), x.

10 Linda M. Austin, "Children of Childhood: Nostalgia and the Romantic Legacy," *Studies in Romanticism*, 42, no. 1 (Spring 2003): 83. I am indebted to the anonymous reader who pointed out the Romantic roots of my concept of aging out of authorship.

11 Robin Bernstein, *Racial Innocence: Performing American Childhood from Slavery to Civil Rights* (New York: New York University Press, 2011).

12 This point about the adult poet's figuration of the self via mourning for childhood is implicit in Austin, "Children of Childhood."

13 Conrad, *Time for Childhoods*, xii. Relevant here is the scholarship on juvenilia, a genre animated by the promise of adult success. In line with this forward-looking energy, Laurie Langbauer's study of Romantic-era white British youth writing theorizes "the juvenile tradition" through the lens of "prolepsis," by which young authors "skip ahead, asserting themselves as writers out of sequence." Whereas Langbauer's subjects essentially borrow power on loan from their privileged adulthoods, the young writers I examine here did not have a bank of adult privilege from which to borrow. Laurie Langbauer, *The Juvenile Tradition: Young Writers and Prolepsis, 1750–1835* (New York: Oxford University Press, 2016), 14.

14 Conrad, *Time for Childhoods*, 1. See also the analysis of *atemporality* in children's stories, the tendency of young writers "to delay, deny and defer the implications of narrative by placing it quite out of time," in Carolyn Steedman, *The Tidy House: Little Girls Writing* (London: Virago, 1982), 106–7. For queer-theoretical analyses of childhood temporality, see Gabrielle Owen, *A Queer History of Adolescence: Developmental Pasts, Relational Futures* (Athens: University of Georgia Press, 2020); Kathryn Bond Stockton, *The Queer Child, or Growing Sideways in the Twentieth Century* (Durham, NC: Duke University Press, 2009).

15 Michael Hanchard, "Afro-Modernity: Temporality, Politics, and the African Diaspora," *Public Culture* 11, no. 1 (January 1999): 253, 256.

16 Daylanne K. English, *Each Hour Redeem: Time and Justice in African American Literature* (Minneapolis: University of Minnesota Press, 2013), 3–4.

17 Martin Luther King, Jr., *The Radical King*, ed. Cornel West (Boston: Beacon Press, 2015), 144.

18 Margo Natalie Crawford, *Black Post-Blackness: The Black Arts Movement and Twenty-First-Century Aesthetics* (Champaign: University of Illinois Press, 2017), 36. Daylanne English offers an alternate reading of time in Black Arts literature, focused on "strategic presentism," an investment to "being in time, being there," fully in the current of revolutionary social and political change. English, *Each Hour Redeem*, 108. While 1960s–1970s child authors indeed deploy such presentism, my analysis here focuses on the anticipatory temporality theorized by Crawford.

19 David Perez, in Young Lords Party and Michael Abramson, *Palante: Young Lords Party* (New York: McGraw-Hill, 1971), 66. See also the analysis of Jim Crow textbook distribution as part of the era's temporal regime of white supremacy, in Stephen Berrey, *The Jim Crow Routine: Everyday Performances of Race, Civil Rights, and Segregation in Mississippi* (Chapel Hill: University of North Carolina Press, 2015), 37.

20 Jonathan Kozol, *Death at an Early Age* (Boston: Houghton Mifflin, 1967).

21 For popular sixth-grade class anthologies, in addition to Mirthes, see Nicholas Anthony Duva, ed., *Somebody Real: Voices of City Children* (Rockaway, NJ: American Faculty Press, 1972); Herbert R. Kohl, *36 Children* (New York: New American Library, 1967).

22 Mirthes and the Children of PS 15, *Can't You Hear Me?*, xii; italics mine.

23 See for instance, Russell Rickford, *We Are an African People* (New York: Oxford University Press, 2016); Michael W. Flamm, *In the Heat of the Summer: The New York Riots of 1964 and the War on Crime* (Philadelphia: University of Pennsylvania Press, 2016); Daniel H. Perlstein, *Justice, Justice: School Politics and the Eclipse of Liberalism*, History of Schools and Schooling (New York: P. Lang, 2004). For accounts of young people's contributions to the era's educational justice movement, see moments throughout Rickford's book; Jesse Hoffnung-Garskof, *A Tale of Two Cities: Santo Domingo and New York after 1950* (Princeton, NJ: Princeton University Press, 2008), 132–62; Amy Fish, "Dreaming 'for Real': June Jordan's *His Own Where* as Youth History," *Lion and the Unicorn* 43, no. 2 (2019): 196–214.

24 Mirthes and the Children of PS 15, *Can't You Hear Me?*, 88.

25 Here I borrow the aptly awkward grammar of "to-be-looked-at-ness" from Laura Mulvey, "Visual Pleasure and Narrative Cinema," *Screen* 16, no. 3 (Autumn 1975): 6–18.

26 Mirthes, introduction to Mirthes and the Children of PS 15, *Can't You Hear Me?*, xi; Carmen, "How Does a Block Swallowed You Up," in Mirthes and the Children of PS 15, *Can't You Hear Me?*, 74.

27 Carmen, "How Does a Block," 74–75.

28 Carmen, "How Does a Block," 74–75.

29 Robert Cooke et al., "Recommendations for a Head Start Program by a Panel of Experts," US Department of Health, Education, and Welfare, 1965.

30 Carmen, "How Does a Block," 75.

31 Mirthes and the Children of PS 15, *Can't You Hear Me?*, 74.

32 Yolanda McDade [Prescott], "The Storm," in *The Children: Poems and Prose from Bedford-Stuyvesant*, ed. Irving Benig (New York: Grove Press, 1971), 89–90. "Yolanda Prescott" is the writer's correct name, as specified in conversation with me.

33 Prescott, "Storm," 89.

34 Prescott, "Storm," 89.

35 Prescott, "Storm," 89.

36 Prescott, "Storm," 89–90.

37 Prescott, "Storm," 90.

38 Yolanda Prescott, conversations and correspondence with author, June 7–11, 2024.

39 Deidre Harris, *Slavery Escape*, in Benig, *Children*, 73.

40 Harris, *Slavery Escape*, 73–74.

41 Harris, *Slavery Escape*, 74–75.

42 Hanchard, "Afro-Modernity," 255.

43 See, for instance, Amiri Baraka's 1967 neo-slave narrative, *Slave Ship: A Historical Pageant*, in Amiri Baraka, *The Motion of History and Other Plays* (New York: William Morrow, 1978), 130–50.

44 Mirthes and the Children of PS 15, *Can't You Hear Me?*, 139–40.

45 June Jordan and Terri Bush, various correspondence, The Voice of the Children collection of Terri Bush, box 3, Schlesinger Library, Harvard University.

46 Benig, preface to Benig, *Children*, vii.

47 I draw here on ideas about teleologies of escape from Katherine Brewer Ball, "Fugitivity," paper presented at The F Words: Flesh, Fantasy, and Fugitivity, symposium at Boston University, Boston, Massachusetts, April 6, 2018.

48 Harris, *Slavery Escape*, 73.

49 Amy Abugo Ongiri, *Spectacular Blackness: The Cultural Politics of the Black Power Movement and the Search for a Black Aesthetic* (Charlottesville: University of Virginia Press, 2010), 19, 23.

50 Larry Neal, "The Black Arts Movement," *Drama Review: TDR* 12, no. 4 (Summer 1968): 32.

51 Irving Benig to Marilyn Meeker, April 24, 1970, Grove Press Records, box 113, Special Collections Research Center, Syracuse University. I am indebted to the Syracuse librarians for their research assistance with these records.

52 Kane, *All Poets Welcome*, 14.

53 Meeker to Benig, April 29, 1970; Benig to Meeker, May 5, 1970, Grove Press Records, box 113.

54 Benig to Meeker, May 5, 1970, Grove Press Records, box 113.

55 Benig to Meeker, October 9, 1970, Grove Press Records, box 113.

56 Although the letter from Thomas is missing from the archive, perhaps because it was written on the same page as the poetic text and thus went to a typist's desk rather than to the editor's files, Meeker did preserve its envelope as well as her own reply to Thomas. Perhaps Meeker found the envelope—addressed to "Miss Marilynn Meeker" with circles dotting the *i*'s and return-addressed to "B'klyn"—charmingly evocative of the book

contributors' youth. Thomas to Meeker, stamped and opened envelope, June 16, 1970, Grove Press Records, box 113.

57 Meeker to Thomas, June 18, 1970, Grove Press Records, box 113.

58 Benig to Meeker, June 15, 1970, Grove Press Records, box 113.

59 Irving Benig, handwritten list of anthology contributors, February 1971, Grove Press Records, box 113. Several names are crossed out; twenty-six are numbered and not crossed out, and Benig is number one.

60 Publishing contract, Grove Press and Irving Benig, 1971, Grove Press Records, box 113.

61 Irving Benig to various [form letters sent to child authors' parents], February 1, 1970, Grove Press Records, box 113.

62 As Meeker wrote to Benig, "All monies shall be paid to you as editor of the book; it will be your responsibility to pay the contributors." Meeker to Benig, January 22, 1971, Grove Press Records, box 113. Benig recalls, "Alas, the book proved a labor of love: it didn't make any money." Though records and memories leave some details unclear, Benig likely paid the children a small amount and personally sponsored some of their activities. Irving Benig, correspondence with the author, May 1, 2024.

63 Back cover to *The Children*, Grove Press Records, box 1085; Grove Press catalog, Spring–Summer 1971, 41, Grove Press Records, box 1085.

64 Benig, foreword to Benig, *Children*, xiii; italics mine.

65 Arnold Shuman to Irving Benig, in Benig, *Children*, 57.

66 Signed parental release forms, February 1, 1970, Grove Press Records, Box 113.

67 Kathy Lawson and Deborah Fulton, untitled exchange, in Benig, *Children*, 69.

68 Odaro (Barbara Jones, slave name), "Alafia," in LeRoi Jones and Larry Neal, eds., *Black Fire: An Anthology of Afro-American Writing* (New York: Morrow, 1968), 356.

69 Conrad, *Time for Childhoods*, 23, 112.

CHAPTER 3

1 C. R. to Mr. Grady, in Stephen M. Joseph, ed., *The Me Nobody Knows: Children's Voices from the Ghetto* (Avon Books, 1969), 52–53; Gary William Friedman, *The Me Nobody Knows* libretto (New York: Sunbeam Music, 1970), act 1, 16. I cite performances in the musical with the act number and the page number in the libretto since scenes are not delineated in this show. I thank Derek Miller for providing insights into the research for this chapter.

2 For a review comparing *The Me* to *Company*, see Emily Genauer, "Giving 4 Cheers for 2 Pairs of Shows," *Newsday*, May 29, 1970.

3 Stephen M. Joseph, introduction to *The Me Nobody Knows*, 10. I use the abbreviation *The Me* to refer only to the musical, not to the anthology.

4 Bruce Weber, "Herb Schapiro, Playwright behind 'The Me Nobody Knows,' Dies at 85," *New York Times*, October 31, 2014.

5 Playbill, "*The Me Nobody Knows*" 7, no. 12 (December 1970): 18; Friedman, *The Me Nobody Knows* libretto.

6 Jerry Parker, "Gathering the 'Me' Almost Nobody Knew," *Newsday*, February 22, 1971.

7 Parker, "Gathering the 'Me.'"

8 Elizabeth Hinton, *From the War on Poverty to the War on Crime: The Making of Mass Incarceration in America* (Cambridge, MA: Harvard University Press, 2016), 219.

9 Kevin Kelly, "Black Who Rode 'the Evil White Horse' Finds Way out of Ghetto," *Boston*

Globe, March 12, 1972. Parker does not mention whether Corbin attended the authors' night.

10 In 2001, at age seventy-eight, Ed Grady told his *The Me* story in an Amazon product review of the musical score. Ed Grady, "Mr. Grady's Feelings about The Me," Amazon product review of *The Me Nobody Knows* musical score, by Gary William Friedman, September 16, 2001, https://www.amazon.com/Me-Nobody-Knows-Will-Holt-ebook /dp/B00Y7PKAOA/ref=sr_1_1?ie=UTF8&qid=1489074334&sr=8-1&keywords=me +nobody+knows. On Grady's career, see "Former Teacher Passes Away," *Hickory Daily Record*, December 13, 2012; "Ed Grady," *IMDb*, http://www.imdb.com/name/nm0333592.

11 Hinton, *War on Poverty*, 218.

12 Karen Sánchez-Eppler, "Marks of Possession: Methods for an Impossible Subject," *PMLA* 126, no. 1 (January 2011): 215; Marah Gubar, "Risky Business: Talking about Children in Children's Literature Criticism," *Children's Literature Association Quarterly* 38, no. 4 (Winter 2013): 453.

13 Robin Bernstein, *Racial Innocence: Performing American Childhood from Slavery to Civil Rights* (New York: New York University Press, 2011). The historical roots of *The Me* also stretch into nineteenth-century popular theater, which, as Marah Gubar has shown, was shaped by children's participation as theatrical creators, cast members, audiences, and taste-makers. Significant to *The Me* is Gubar's claim that mixed-age spaces of performance have historically staged encounters between constructed ideals of childhood and the lived realities of poor and working-class children and children of color: that is, the paradoxes of childhood in an unjust nation. Marah Gubar, "Entertaining Children of All Ages: Nineteenth-Century Popular Theater as Children's Theater," *American Quarterly* 66, no. 1 (March 2014): 1–34.

14 Allison Curseen argues for the potent role of children, specifically Black girls, within fugitivity studies in "Black Girlish Departure and the 'Semiotics of Theater' in Harriet Jacobs's Narrative; or, Lulu & Ellen: Four Opening Acts," *Theatre Survey* 60, no. 1 (January 2019): 91–121. Also relevant here are analyses of Black children's mobility, particularly Jayna Brown, *Babylon Girls: Black Women Performers and the Shaping of the Modern* (Durham, NC: Duke University Press, 2008); Crystal Lynn Webster, *Beyond the Boundaries of Childhood: African American Children in the Antebellum North* (Chapel Hill: University of North Carolina Press, 2021); Allison Curseen, "'Everything Is Alive': Moving and Reading in Excess of American Freedom," *American Literature* 90, no. 1 (March 2018): 83–109.

15 Josephine Lee, "Racial Actors, Liberal Myths," *Xcp: Cross-Cultural Poetics*, no. 13 (2003): 93. On the racial dynamics of casting, see also Brian Eugenio Herrera, *Latin Numbers: Playing Latino in Twentieth-Century U.S. Popular Performance* (Ann Arbor: University of Michigan Press, 2015); Angela Pao, *No Safe Spaces: Re-Casting Race, Ethnicity, and Nationality in American Theater* (Ann Arbor: University of Michigan Press, 2010); Brandi Wilkins Catanese, *The Problem of the Color[blind]: Racial Transgression and the Politics of Black Performance* (Ann Arbor: University of Michigan Press, 2011).

16 Ju Yon Kim, "Between Paper and Performance: Suspicion, Race, and Casting in *The Piano Teacher*," *Modern Drama* 63, no. 2 (Summer 2020): 127–53.

17 Michael J. Dumas and Joseph Derrick Nelson, "(Re)Imagining Black Boyhood: Toward a Critical Framework for Educational Research," *Harvard Educational Review* 86, no. 1 (March 2016): 27–47; Simone C. Drake, "A Meditation on the Soundscapes of Black Boyhood and Disruptive Imaginations," *Souls* 18, no. 2–4 (October 2016): 446–58.

18 "Mississippi Goddam," track 7 on Nina Simone, *Nina Simone in Concert*, recorded at

Carnegie Hall, March–April 1964, Phillips, 1964. I draw here on the reading in Daphne A. Brooks, "Nina Simone's Triple Play," *Callaloo* 34, no. 1 (Winter 2011): 187.

19 On the Youth House system, see, for instance, Robert Daley, "Youth House Acts to Drop Jail Aura," *New York Times*, October 2, 1964; Larry Cole, *Street Kids* (New York: Grossman, 1970), 56–59.

20 Will Holt et al., "First Draft" of "The Me Nobody Knows," annotated typescript, 1970, Billy Rose Theatre Division, New York Public Library, New York.

21 C. R.'s letters to Grady appear in Joseph, *The Me Nobody Knows*, 52–58, and in the musical libretto, Friedman, *The Me Nobody Knows* libretto, act 1, 16; act 1, 21–22; act 2, 13; act 2, 21. Because this section discusses parts of C. R.'s letters that are adapted into the musical and other parts that are not used in the musical, I cite subsequent passages from the letters with page numbers of *The Me Nobody Knows* anthology, rather than *The Me* libretto. At times, the libretto makes minor adjustments to the anthologized texts, such as changing comma placements or adding single words; I quote the anthologized version of the texts.

22 The epistolary musical surged in popularity in the 1990s and continues to structure some of the most popular Broadway shows of the twenty-first century, including *Hamilton* (2015) and *Dear Evan Hansen* (2015). For an analysis of one influential epistolary musical, Stephen Sondheim's *Passion* (1994), see Raymond Knapp, *The American Musical and the Performance of Personal Identity* (Princeton, NJ: Princeton University Press, 2010), 303–5.

23 C. R. to Grady, in Joseph, *The Me Nobody Knows*, 52, 54, 55.

24 C. R. to Grady, in Joseph, *The Me Nobody Knows*, 57.

25 C. R. to Grady, in Joseph, *The Me Nobody Knows*, 57.

26 C. R. to Grady, in Joseph, *The Me Nobody Knows*, 53.

27 C. R. to Grady, in Joseph, *The Me Nobody Knows*, 52, 58.

28 Lee Bernstein, "Prison Writers and the Black Arts Movement," in *New Thoughts on the Black Arts Movement*, ed. Lisa Gail Collins and Margo Natalie Crawford (New Brunswick, NJ: Rutgers University Press, 2006), 312; Piri Thomas, interview by Carmen Dolores Hernández, in *Puerto Rican Voices in English: Interviews with Writers*, ed. Carmen Dolores Hernández (Westport, Conn.: Praeger, 1997), 179.

29 Akmir-U-Akbar, "The Transformation," in Joseph, *The Me Nobody Knows*, 45; Friedman, *The Me Nobody Knows* libretto, act 1, 17.

30 Akmir-U-Akbar, "The Transformation," in Joseph, *The Me Nobody Knows*, 45; Friedman, *The Me Nobody Knows* libretto, act 1, 17.

31 "New Paperbacks: Children Say It with Love," unsigned review column, *Boston Globe*, September 10, 1971.

32 Franz Kafka, *Metamorphosis*, 1915, trans. David Wyllie, 2002 (Project Gutenberg, 2012), https://www.gutenberg.org/files/5200/5200-h/5200-h.htm; Akmir-U-Akbar, "The Transformation," in Joseph, *The Me Nobody Knows*, 45; Friedman, *The Me Nobody Knows* libretto, act 1, 17.

33 Robin D. G. Kelley, *Yo' Mama's Disfunktional! Fighting the Culture Wars in Urban America* (Boston: Beacon Press, 1997), 20.

34 Akmir-U-Akbar, "The Transformation," in Joseph, *The Me Nobody Knows*, 45; Friedman, *The Me Nobody Knows* libretto, act 1, 17.

35 Elaine Avidon, Zoom conversation with author, February 22, 2024; Elaine Avidon, correspondence with author, January 30, 2024, and February 28, 2024. On the influence of What's Happening (sometimes referenced with a question mark, as "What's Happening?"), see Herbert Kohl, interview by Phillip Lopate, in *Journal of a Living Experiment: A*

Documentary History of the First Ten Years of Teachers and Writers Collaborative, ed. Phillip Lopate (New York: Teachers and Writers Collaborative, 1979), 23; Barbara Falconer, "The Young View . . . 'I'm Black!'" *Look*, January 7, 1969, pp. 12–13. Uniquely in *The Me Nobody Knows* anthology, all texts written by What's Happening members are stated as copyrighted to the group because the works were previously published in the magazine.

36 Joseph, *The Me Nobody Knows*, 45.

37 Alondra Nelson, *Body and Soul: The Black Panther Party and the Fight against Medical Discrimination* (Minneapolis: University of Minnesota Press, 2011), 20; Alondra Nelson, "A Black Mass as Black Gothic: Myth and Bioscience in Black Cultural Nationalism," in Collins and Crawford, *New Thoughts*, 139.

38 Friedman, *The Me Nobody Knows* libretto, act 1, 17.

39 Herbert Blau, *Take Up the Bodies: Theater at the Vanishing Point* (Champaign: University of Illinois Press, 1982), 83.

40 Ralph Ellison, *Invisible Man* (New York: Vintage, 1980), 3, 581. See Hortense J. Spillers, "Ellison's 'Usable Past': Toward a Theory of Myth," in *Black, White, and in Color: Essays on American Literature and Culture* (Chicago, IL: University of Chicago Press, 2003), 78.

41 C. M., "The Hopeless Tree," in Joseph, *The Me Nobody Knows*, 125.

42 Shel Silverstein, *The Giving Tree* (New York: Harper & Row, 1964).

43 Jonathan Kozol, *Death at an Early Age* (Boston: Houghton Mifflin, 1967), 77, 74.

44 Mason Locke Weems, *The Life of George Washington*, Internet Archive 2011 (Philadelphia, PA: Lippincott, 1800), 15–16, http://archive.org/details/lifeofgeorgewashweem.

45 Assata Shakur, *Assata: An Autobiography* (Westport, CT: L. Hill, 1987), 32–33.

46 "The Tree" is sung in act 2, 7. Will Holt's first draft of the script calls for "SONG: THE HOPELESS TREE (ballad)" to be "sung by Mr. Grady letter writer," as indeed it would be. Curtis M's story is pasted here in the script, though with a pink marker scratch-out over it, and does not yet appear as an epigraph. Holt, "First Draft."

47 Friedman, *The Me Nobody Knows* libretto, act 2, 6. Clorox here performs Tim Engel's piece "On Broadway," in Joseph, *The Me Nobody Knows*, 73–74.

48 Friedman, *The Me Nobody Knows* libretto, act 2, 7.

49 Daphne Brooks, *Bodies in Dissent: Spectacular Performances of Race and Freedom, 1850–1910* (Durham, NC: Duke University Press, 2006), 8, quoting Saidiya V. Hartman, *Scenes of Subjection: Terror, Slavery, and Self-Making in Nineteenth-Century America* (New York: Oxford University Press, 1997), 36. On the African American literary trope of the veil, see Cynthia D. Schrager, "Both Sides of the Veil: Race, Science, and Mysticism in W. E. B. Du Bois," *American Quarterly* 48, no. 4 (December 1996): 551–86.

50 Brian Eugenio Herrera, "There Is Power in Casting," *Youth Theatre Journal* 29 (2015): 147.

51 Holt, "First Draft."

52 This approximate breakdown of gendered authorship almost certainly elides the gender identities of some of the young writers of *The Me*. I counted each text separately, even if multiple texts appeared by the same author, except in the case of the C. R. letters—examined later in this chapter—which I counted as a single male-authored text. For those texts that I counted as male-authored or female-authored, I assumed the normative gendering of first names. Some texts were prefaced by editorial comments by Joseph that used gender pronouns. Those texts that I classified as containing male-identified language included, for instance, cases in which the poetic speaker identifies as a "brother" or as part of "us boys." Although a poetic speaker may certainly perform a gender identity different from that of the author, I estimate the majority of such texts were written by boys. Finally,

I counted texts with no obvious gendering; many texts in the anthology either contain no byline or are signed only with the author's initials and age. The predominance of male-authored texts could be due to any combination of Joseph's preferences as an editor, the preferences of teachers in saving and sharing children's writings, and the gendering of certain classrooms and groups from whose teachers Joseph collected texts. For instance, the writings from Youth House residents may have been drawn from all-male classes, since Youth House held both boys and girls but was largely gender-segregated.

53 Brian Herrera, "The Best Actor for the Role, or the Mythos of Casting in American Popular Performance," *Journal of American Drama and Theatre* 27, no. 2 (Spring 2015): 1–11.

54 Martha Knight, "Production Notes," in Friedman, *The Me Nobody Knows* libretto, n.p.

55 Quoted in Catanese, *Problem of the Color[blind]*, 15; italics mine. See the discussion of Simon's praise for *The Me* in chapter 4.

56 Joseph, introduction to *The Me Nobody Knows*, 9.

57 Knight, "Character Breakdown" and "Production Notes," in Friedman, *The Me Nobody Knows* libretto, n.p.

58 While several contributors write explicitly about Black identity, such as in the poem that inspires *The Me*'s song "Black," other writers implicitly address race and racism. Regarding shifts to the script to accommodate actors, it is possible that speeches could be changed to accommodate Asian American, Native American, or other minority actors, but such possibilities do not seem to be part of Knight's calculus here. Likewise, the show could have created more than one Latino or Latina role and shown a greater diversity of Latinx identities.

59 Herrera, *Latin Numbers*, 4–5.

60 Parker, "Gathering the 'Me.'"

61 Parker, "Gathering the 'Me.'"

62 Jack Stillinger, *Multiple Authorship and the Myth of Solitary Genius* (New York: Oxford University Press, 1991), 174.

63 Parker, "Gathering the 'Me.'"

64 Parker, "Gathering the 'Me.'"

65 Friedman, *The Me Nobody Knows* libretto, act 1, 6; from N. W. [Harry Wescott], untitled ["Windy windy windy skys"], in Joseph, *The Me Nobody Knows*, 95.

66 Friedman, *The Me Nobody Knows* libretto, act 1, 6.

67 Kelly, "Black Who Rode."

CHAPTER 4

1 Warren Doty, Samuel Robinson, and students, "Straight Talk from Teenagers," *Somebody Turned on a Tap in These Kids: Poetry and Young People Today*, ed. Nancy Larrick (New York: Delacorte Press, 1971), 98–99. The student speaking is Romani Wardlaw, Veronica West, or James Heath, Juan Dawson's fellow students on the panel. The transcriber presumably did not recognize the voice of the student speaking at this moment in the audio recording.

2 June Jordan, "Children and the Hungering For," in Larrick, *Somebody Turned a Tap*, 63.

3 Sell, *Avant-Garde Performance*, 5.

4 Jodi Melamed, *Represent and Destroy: Rationalizing Violence in the New Racial Capitalism* (Minneapolis: University of Minnesota Press, 2011), 16. See also Roderick A. Ferguson, *The Reorder of Things: The University and Its Pedagogies of Minority Difference*

(Minneapolis: University of Minnesota Press, 2012); Mark McGurl, *The Program Era: Postwar Fiction and the Rise of Creative Writing* (Cambridge, MA: Harvard University Press, 2009).

5 Melamed, *Represent and Destroy*, 37.

6 W. K. Wimsatt and M. C. Beardsley, "The Intentional Fallacy," *Sewanee Review* 54, no. 3 (Summer 1946): 476.

7 Hughes Mearns, *Creative Youth: How a School Environment Set Free the Creative Spirit* (Garden City, NY: Doubleday, Page, 1925).

8 Sell, *Avant-Garde Performance*, 243.

9 Phillip Lopate, "Issues of Language," in *Journal of a Living Experiment: A Documentary History of the First Ten Years of Teachers and Writers Collaborative*, ed. Phillip Lopate (New York: Teachers and Writers Collaborative, 1979), 100.

10 Patrick Groff, "Where Are We Going with Poetry for Children?," *Horn Book* 42 (August 1966): 458–59, 462.

11 B. Jo Kinnick, review of *I Heard a Scream in the Street*, ed. Nancy Larrick, *English Journal* 60, no. 6 (September 1971): 823.

12 Peter F. Neumeyer, review of *The Voice of the Children*, ed. June Jordan and Terri Bush, *Teachers College Record* 73, no. 1 (September 1971): 150, 151.

13 Ruth Kearney Carlson, "The Creative Thrust of Poetry Writing," *Elementary English* 49, no. 8 (1972): 1177; John Simon, "The 'Me' You Must Get to Know," *New York Magazine*, n.d. [Summer–Fall 1970]; William Leonard, "'The Me Nobody Knows' a Hit," *Chicago Tribune*, February 20, 1971.

14 Gerald Graff, "What Was New Criticism? Literary Interpretation and Scientific Objectivity," *Salmagundi* 27 (1974): 73.

15 Myra Cohn Livingston, "What the Heart Knows Today," in Larrick, *Somebody Turned on a Tap*, 8.

16 Patrick Groff, review of *Somebody Real: Voices of City Children*, ed. Nicholas Anthony Duva, *The Reading Teacher* 27, no. 1 (1973): 107–8.

17 Susan Sontag, *Against Interpretation and Other Essays* (New York: Farrar, Straus and Giroux, 2013), 16.

18 Robin Bernstein, *Racial Innocence: Performing American Childhood from Slavery to Civil Rights* (New York: New York University Press, 2011), 7.

19 June Jordan and Terri Bush, eds., *The Voice of the Children* (New York: Holt, Rinehart and Winston, 1970).

20 John Simon, "The 'Me' You Must Get to Know"; Martin Washburn, "Theater: The Me Nobody Knows," *Village Voice*, May 28, 1970; Bob Micklin, "Road to Success through the Ghetto," *Newsday*, September 14, 1970.

21 Leonard, "'The Me Nobody Knows' a Hit."

22 Richard L. Coe, "'The Me Nobody Knows': Harsh Realities, Privileged Hope," *Washington Post*, August 17, 1971.

23 Martin Washburn, "Theater: The Me Nobody Knows"; Eve Merriam, "For Young Readers," *New York Times*, January 24, 1971.

24 Edith Oliver, "Off Broadway: Rejoice," *New Yorker*, May 30, 1970.

25 Quoted in in Henry Louis Gates, *The Trials of Phillis Wheatley: America's First Black Poet and Her Encounters with the Founding Fathers* (New York: Basic Civitas Books, 2003), 42.

26 For a typical brief write-up in this mode, see "Children's Poems in Paperback," *Baltimore Sun*, January 10, 1971.

27 Margaret Mead and James Baldwin, *A Rap on Race* (Philadelphia: J. B. Lippincott, 1971), 72–73.

28 Jane D. Vreeland, review of *The Me Nobody Knows; I Am Somebody; From a Busy Hubbub, Elementary English* 48, no. 7 (1971): 887–89.

29 Mary Anne Hall and Linda B. Gambrell, "Children as Authors," review of *The Voice of the Children*, ed. June Jordan and Terri Bush, *Elementary English* 49, no. 6 (1972): 892.

30 Jean McClellan, "The Children's Page," *Elementary English* 50, no. 6 (September 1973): 963. The column ran from 1972 to 1976.

31 Linnea Lilja, "Anthologies of Children's Writing," *English Education* 6, no. 3 (February–March 1975): 178; Abraham Willard, "'Free' Curriculum Releases Students," *Arizona Republic*, June 3, 1973; Kinnick, review of *I Heard a Scream in the Street*, 824.

32 Marvin Hoffman, "The Other Mouth: Writing in the Schools," *Childhood Education* 47, no. 2 (November 1970): 82.

33 Carlson, "Creative Thrust," 1185; Nancy Larrick, "Pop/Rock Lyrics, Poetry and Reading," *Journal of Reading* 15, no. 3 (December 1971): 188; Art Berger, "Poet in the School house: Evoking Creative Energy in Language" (speech transcript, Annual Convention of the National Council of Teachers of English, November 1970), ERIC, https://eric.ed.gov /?q=ED051235&id=ED051235; italics mine. For further characterizations of youth writing as *bitter*, see Lilja, "Anthologies of Children's Writing," 181; Kinnick, review of *I Heard a Scream in the Street*, 824; unsigned review of *A Screaming Whisper* by Vanessa Howard, *Sun Reporter* (San Francisco, CA), August 25, 1973.

34 Martin Luther King, Jr., "The Violence of Desperate Men," in *The Radical King*, ed. Cornel West (Boston, MA: Beacon Press, 2015), 11.

35 Carlson, "Creative Thrust," 1185, 1186.

36 Neumeyer, review of *The Voice of the Children*, 152.

37 Catherine Mackintosh, "A Study of Publishing Trends in Available Anthologies of Poetry for Children Published in 1950–1970" (master's thesis, Southern Connecticut State College, 1972), 78. For further references to "freshness," see the approval of moments of "childlike freshness" in Groff, review of *Somebody Real*; Nancy Larrick, ed., *Green Is Like a Meadow of Grass: An Anthology of Children's Pleasure in Poetry* (Champaign, IL: Garrard, 1968), 63.

38 Lopate, "Issues of Language," 112. My interest in political embarrassment here is inspired by but distinct from that discussed in Lauren Berlant, "'68, or Something," *Critical Inquiry* 21, no. 1 (Autumn 1994): 124–55.

39 Jordan, "Children and the Hungering For," 56, 57.

40 June Jordan, *Who Look at Me* (New York: Thomas Y. Crowell, 1969).

41 Kevin Quashie and Amy Fish, "A Subjunctive Imagining: June Jordan's *Who Look at Me* and the Conditions of Black Agency," in *Literary Cultures and Twentieth-Century Childhoods*, ed. Rachel Conrad and L. Brown Kennedy (New York: Routledge, 2020), 55. Richard Flynn points to the connections among the Voice of the Children, *Who Look at Me*, and Poetry for the People in Flynn, "'Affirmative Acts': Language, Childhood, and Power in June Jordan's Cross-Writing," *Children's Literature* 30, no. 1 (2002): 159–85.

42 June Jordan, introduction to *June Jordan's Poetry for the People: A Revolutionary Blueprint*, ed. Jordan Muller and Blueprint Collective (New York: Routledge, 1995), 3.

43 Jordan, introduction to *June Jordan's Poetry*, 8.

44 Jordan, introduction to *June Jordan's Poetry*, 8; italics mine.

EPILOGUE

1 June Jordan, "To Be Black and Female," review of *Black Macho and the Myth of the Super-woman*, by Michele Wallace, *New York Times*, March 18, 1979.

2 W. N., "Jail-Life Walk," in *The Me Nobody Knows: Children's Voices from the Ghetto*, ed. Stephen Joseph (New York: Avon Books, 1969), 33. I saw *Notes from the Field* at the American Repertory Theatre, Cambridge, Massachusetts, August 27, 2016, as well as on film after its HBO release. The show was staged off-Broadway with Second Stage Theater in 2016 and was performed in other cities as well.

3 Anna Deavere Smith, *Notes from the Field* (New York: Anchor, 2019), 116–17. Smith lightly alters and rearranges Baldwin's wording for the purposes of her monologue; I have quoted from Smith's published script here. Ellipses are mine, though Smith has also trimmed Baldwin's original, which is printed in Margaret Mead and James Baldwin, *A Rap on Race* (Philadelphia: J. B. Lippincott, 1971), 172–73.

4 W. N., "Jail-Life Walk," in Joseph, *The Me Nobody Knows*, 33. As a Youth House resident, W. N. may have worked with teacher Ed Grady, discussed in chapter 3. *The Way It Spozed to Be* is a 1968 memoir of junior high school teaching that barely quotes students. Baldwin's conflation of the two books suggests that he may have read deeply in the genres of teacher memoirs and youth writing collections. James Herndon, *The Way It Spozed to Be* (New York: Simon and Schuster, 1968).

5 W. N., "Jail-Life Walk," in Joseph, *The Me Nobody Knows*, 33.

6 See, for instance, Negley K. Teeters, "State of Prisons in the United States: 1870–1970," *Federal Probation* 33 (1969): 22.

7 W. N., "Jail-Life Walk," in Joseph, *The Me Nobody Knows*, 33.

8 "Write the Future: A 20th Anniversary Celebration," 826 NYC, 2024, https://826nyc.org /event_826/write-the-future-a-20th-anniversary-celebration; "Our Program," National Youth Poet Laureate Program, 2022, https://www.youthlaureate.org.

9 Amanda Holpuch, "Florida School Restricts Access to Amanda Gorman's Inauguration Poem," *New York Times*, May 24, 2023. The school removed the book from library shelves accessible to K–5 grade students, placing it within a media center that could be accessed only by students in grades 6–8. The parent's complaint echoes indoctrination accusations leveled against the Black Panther Party's Free Breakfast for Children program and other children's programs of the 1960s and 1970s.

10 Amanda Gorman (@amandascgorman), "So they ban my book . . . ," Instagram, May 23, 2023, https://www.instagram.com/p/CsmfbFWypgC/.

11 Kasey Meehan and Jonathan Friedman, "2023 Banned Books Update: Banned in the USA," PEN America, April 20, 2023, https://pen.org/report/banned-in-the-usa-state -laws-supercharge-book-suppression-in-schools/.

Index

Page numbers followed by an f indicate a figure.